Psychology of Skill Development:

A Counselling-Centric Approach for Student Growth and Employability

Psychology of Skill Development

Published By: Wissira Research Lab

Imprint Name: Wissira Press

US Office: Carmel, United States- 46074

India Office: KDP, RNE, India-201017

Email: editor@wissira.us, Website: https://books.wissira.us

Mobile: +91 7535 916 555

Kishore Raipurkar

ISBN - 978-93-7559-243-3

Maharaja Agrasen Himalayan Garhwal University,

Address: Uttarakhand, India

Edition: 2026

Printed In: India

A Counselling-Centric Approach for Student Growth and Employability

Maharaja Agrasen Himalayan Garhwal University,

Address: Uttarakhand, India

Psychology of Skill Development:

A Counselling-Centric Approach for Student Growth and Employability

2026

Author:

Kishore Raipurkar

Published By

Wissira Research Lab

ISBN 978-93-7559-243-3

9 789375 592433

Preface

In an era defined by rapid technological change, evolving career landscapes, and increasing psychological demands on learners, the concept of skill development can no longer be limited to technical proficiency alone. Students today are expected not only to acquire knowledge but also to adapt, communicate, manage emotions, think critically, and remain resilient in the face of continuous change. These expectations call for a deeper understanding of the psychological foundations that shape learning, performance, and employability. This book, *Psychology of Skill Development: A Counselling-Centric Approach for Student Growth and Employability*, is written in response to this need.

The central premise of this work is that skill development is fundamentally a psychological process. Every skill—whether cognitive, emotional, social, or vocational—emerges from the interaction between the mind, brain, environment, and personal experience. Traditional education systems often emphasize outcomes while overlooking the internal barriers students face, such as fear of failure, low self-confidence, emotional stress, or lack of direction. By placing counselling at the core of skill development, this book seeks to bridge the gap between potential and performance.

This transition from "learning to earning" is rarely a linear path; it is a psychological transition that requires a robust internal locus of control. As industries are disrupted by automation and artificial intelligence, the ability to manage the cognitive load of upskilling becomes a vital competency in itself. This book argues that being "job-ready" must be preceded by being "psychologically ready"—having the mental fortitude to pivot when career trajectories shift unexpectedly. By examining the neuroplasticity that allows for lifelong mastery, we can see that learning is as much an emotional endeavour as it is a physiological one.

This volume integrates insights from educational psychology, counselling psychology, neuroscience, and career development studies to present a holistic framework for student growth. It explores how motivation, self-awareness, emotional intelligence, resilience, and biological mechanisms influence the acquisition and mastery of skills. At the same time, it highlights the practical role of counsellors, educators, and mentors in guiding learners through these complex processes. It emphasizes that academic success is often the byproduct of mental well-being; when students possess the self-regulatory tools to navigate anxiety, they are far more likely to translate their technical knowledge into professional impact.

The book is intended for educators, counsellors, teacher trainees, psychologists, higher education professionals, and students who wish to understand not just what skills are needed, but how they are developed and sustained. By emphasizing reflection, emotional readiness, and lifelong learning, this work aims to contribute to a more humane, inclusive, and effective approach to education and employability. Ultimately, this approach moves away from a transactional view of education toward a transformational one, where vulnerability is seen as a precursor to learning rather than a weakness.

It is hoped that this book will encourage readers to view skill development as a journey of self-discovery and psychological growth—one that empowers students to navigate learning and careers with confidence, adaptability, and purpose. By fostering environments that prioritize psychological safety, we can ensure that growth is not just efficient, but deeply sustainable for the challenges of tomorrow.

Authors:

Kishore Raipurkar

Overview of the Book

Psychology of Skill Development: A Counselling-Centric Approach for Student Growth and Employabilit y offers a comprehensive and integrated exploration of how skills are formed, strengthened, and sustained through psychological processes. The book moves beyond the conventional focus on technical training and presents skill development as a multidimensional journey shaped by cognition, emotion, biology, social interaction, and purposeful guidance.

The opening chapters lay the conceptual foundation by explaining the meaning and evolution of skill development from a psychological perspective. They emphasize the importance of understanding the student mind-cognitively, emotionally, and socially-before attempting any form of skill training. Motivation, learning styles, and psychological diversity are presented as key determinants of how effectively students engage with skill acquisition.

Subsequent chapters focus on internal capacities that shape skill identity and performance. Self-awareness, emotional intelligence, and confidence are explored as essential building blocks for sustainable learning and employability. The book highlights how counselling enables students to identify strengths, address limitations, regulate emotions, and align skills with personal values and career aspirations.

The middle sections examine cognitive and social skills, critical thinking, communication, resilience, and adaptability. These chapters demonstrate how psychological readiness influences performance in academic settings and real-world environments. Practical examples and counselling-oriented explanations illustrate how students can overcome fear, stress, and self-doubt while developing higher-order skills.

The later chapters extend the discussion to employability, future skills, and lifelong learning. They address the psychological demands of career transitions, industry expectations, and continuous skill renewal in a rapidly changing world. The biological foundations of skill development and the structured progression outlined in Bloom's Taxonomy provide scientific grounding for understanding how skills evolve from basic competence to expertise.

Core Philosophy

The central thesis of this book is that **counselling is the bridge between potential and performance.** Before a student can master a technical skill, they must first navigate the internal landscape of their own mind. By integrating psychological insights with practical guidance, this book empowers educators and learners to address the "hidden" barriers to success—such as fear of failure and emotional dysregulation.

Structural Journey of the Book

- **The Conceptual Foundation (Chapters 1–3):** The opening chapters establish why we must understand the student mind—cognitively and emotionally—before training begins. It explores how motivation and psychological diversity act as the primary engines for effective learning.
- **Internal Building Blocks (Chapters 4–6):** Focus shifts to the "inner architecture" of success. This section examines how **Self-Awareness** and **Emotional Intelligence** form a student's "Skill Identity," allowing them to align their talents with their career aspirations through the lens of counselling.

Overall, the book presents a cohesive framework that positions counselling as a central pillar of education and skill development. It advocates for learner-centric, psychologically informed practices that empower students to grow not only as skilled professionals, but also as confident, resilient, and adaptable individuals prepared for lifelong learning and meaningful careers.

Table of Contents

1

Introduction to Skill Development Psychology

1.1 Meaning and Evolution of Skill Development

Skill development refers to the gradual process through which individuals acquire, refine, and master abilities that enable effective performance in academic, professional, and social contexts. Historically, skills were viewed as fixed traits-either possessed or absent.

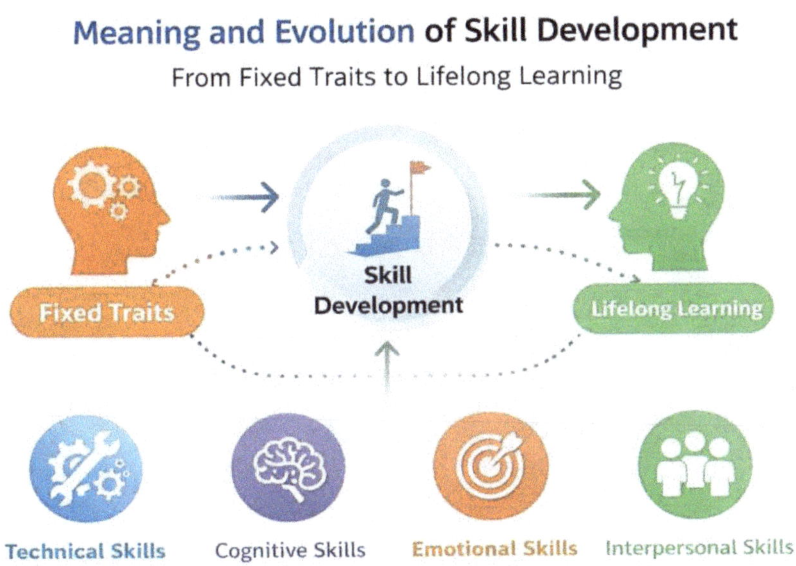

Skill development can be understood as a continuous and lifelong process through which individuals learn, improve, and adapt their abilities to meet personal, academic, professional, and social demands. Rather than being a one-time achievement, it involves repeated practice, exposure to new situations, and conscious efforts to improve performance over time. Skills enable individuals to apply knowledge effectively, solve problems, communicate clearly, and respond appropriately to changing environments.

In earlier periods, skills were often considered **innate or fixed qualities** . People were believed to be naturally talented or untalented in specific areas, with limited scope for improvement. This view dominated traditional education systems, where success was attributed largely to inborn intelligence or natural aptitude. However, advancements in psychology and education challenged this assumption by demonstrating that abilities can be shaped and strengthened through learning and experience.

With the rise of behavioural and cognitive psychology, skills came to be seen as **learned behaviours and mental processes** . Researchers emphasized the role of practice, reinforcement, observation, and feedback in shaping human capabilities. Learning theories highlighted that individuals develop skills through interaction with their environment rather than through heredity alone.

In contemporary understanding, skill development is viewed as a **dynamic and holistic process**. It encompasses not only technical or vocational abilities but also cognitive skills such as critical thinking, emotional skills like self-regulation, and people skills such as teamwork and empathy. Modern perspectives stress reflection, adaptability, and lifelong learning, recognizing skill development as essential for personal growth, employability, and effective participation in society.

1.2 Psychological Skills vs. Technical Skills

Technical skills involve task-specific knowledge such as operating tools, using software, or applying procedures. Psychological skills, in contrast, govern *how* individuals learn, adapt, persist, and perform under pressure. These include attention control, emotional regulation, motivation, decision-making, and resilience.

Technical skills refer to **task-oriented and domain-specific abilities** required to perform particular activities effectively. These include operating machinery, using digital tools, applying mathematical or scientific procedures, and following standardized methods within a profession. Such skills are usually acquired through formal training, instruction, or firsthand practice and are often measurable through tests, certifications, or performance outcomes. Technical skills are essential for entry into academic programs, trades, or professional roles because they demonstrate functional competence.

Psychological skills, on the other hand, relate to the **internal processes that shape how individuals apply their knowledge and abilities**. These skills influence learning capacity, adaptability, and performance consistency across situations. They include attention control, emotional regulation, self-motivation, decision-making under uncertainty, perseverance, and resilience in the face of challenges. Psychological skills are not tied to a single task or profession; instead, they operate across contexts and determine how effectively individuals respond to pressure, setbacks, and change.

While technical skills can enable individuals to **perform specific tasks**, psychological skills determine **how well and how sustainably those tasks are performed**. A person may possess strong technical knowledge but struggle with anxiety, low motivation, or poor self-regulation, leading to inconsistent outcomes. In contrast, individuals with well-developed psychological skills can adapt their technical abilities to new situations, learn from feedback, and maintain performance over time.

From the perspective of skill development psychology, long-term success depends on the **integration of both skill types**. Technical competence provides capability, but psychological readiness ensures stability, growth, and effective application. Without psychological skills, technical expertise often remains underused or fails to translate into consistent real-world performance.

1.3 Skill Development as a Cognitive and Emotional Process

Skill acquisition is not merely mechanical repetition; it involves deep cognitive processing and emotional engagement. Learners must understand concepts, manage frustration, tolerate mistakes, and sustain effort over time. Emotions such as confidence, anxiety, and interest significantly influence learning speed and retention.

Skill development extends far beyond simple repetition of actions or routines; it is a **complex cognitive and emotional process** that unfolds over time. At the cognitive level, learners must comprehend underlying concepts, recognize patterns, apply reasoning, and adjust strategies based on feedback. Effective skill acquisition requires attention, memory, problem-solving, and reflection, allowing individuals to move from basic understanding to confident application.

Equally important is the **emotional dimension of learning**. As individuals acquire new skills, they inevitably encounter errors, slow progress, and moments of self-doubt. Emotions such as frustration, anxiety, and disappointment can either hinder or motivate learning, depending on how they are managed. Conversely, positive emotions like curiosity, confidence, and interest enhance engagement, persistence, and the willingness to practice. Emotional responses strongly influence how long learners sustain effort and how effectively they retain what they learn.

Psychological research highlights the role of **belief systems** in shaping skill development. Self-efficacy-one's belief in the ability to succeed-affects how challenges are approached and how setbacks are interpreted. Learners who view ability as developable are more likely to persist, seek feedback, and improve, while those with fixed beliefs may withdraw when faced with difficulty.

Therefore, skill development is best understood as an **integrated interaction between cognition and emotion**. Learning progresses not in a straight line but through cycles of understanding, effort, emotional regulation, and adaptation. Recognizing this integration helps explain why supportive environments, constructive feedback, and emotional awareness are essential for sustainable and meaningful skill acquisition.

Example: Skill Development as a Cognitive and Emotional Process

Consider a student learning **public speaking**. Cognitively, the student must understand how to structure a speech, organize ideas logically, choose appropriate language, and remember key points while speaking. This involves attention, memory, and reasoning skills. Simply memorizing a speech without understanding its flow often leads to confusion or breakdown during delivery.

At the same time, the student experiences strong **emotional responses**. Initial attempts may trigger anxiety, fear of judgment, or frustration after making mistakes. If the student believes that "I am bad at speaking," these emotions may reduce motivation and practice time. However, with positive feedback, gradual exposure, and growing self-confidence, emotions such as interest and pride begin to replace fear.

Over time, as the student manages nervousness, accepts mistakes as part of learning, and builds self-efficacy, performance improves. The technical aspects of speaking become smoother because emotional regulation supports sustained effort and concentration.

This example shows that successful skill development occurs when cognitive understanding and emotional management work together , rather than through practice alone.

1.4 Role of Counselling in Modern Education

Counselling plays a foundational role in skill development by addressing internal barriers that traditional instruction overlooks. Counsellors help students clarify goals, manage emotional challenges, build confidence, and develop realistic self-perceptions.

Counselling plays a crucial and foundational role in modern skill education by addressing the psychological and emotional factors that traditional teaching methods often fail to consider. While classroom instruction and training programs focus primarily on content delivery and technical competence, counselling supports the learner's internal readiness to learn, adapt, and apply skills effectively.

One of the key contributions of counselling is goal clarification . Many learners struggle not because of a lack of ability, but due to unclear direction or unrealistic expectations. Counsellors help students identify their strengths, interests, and limitations, enabling them to set achievable and meaningful goals. This clarity improves motivation and commitment to skill-building activities.

Counselling also assists learners in managing emotional challenges such as anxiety, fear of failure, low self-esteem, and stress. These emotional barriers can significantly hinder learning and performance. Through reflective dialogue and psychological support, counsellors help individuals develop confidence, resilience, and healthier responses to setbacks.

Furthermore, counselling encourages **self-awareness and reflective learning**. Learners gain insight into their learning styles, belief systems, and behavioural patterns, allowing them to adapt strategies that suit their personal needs. As a result, skill development becomes an active and personalized process rather than passive instruction.

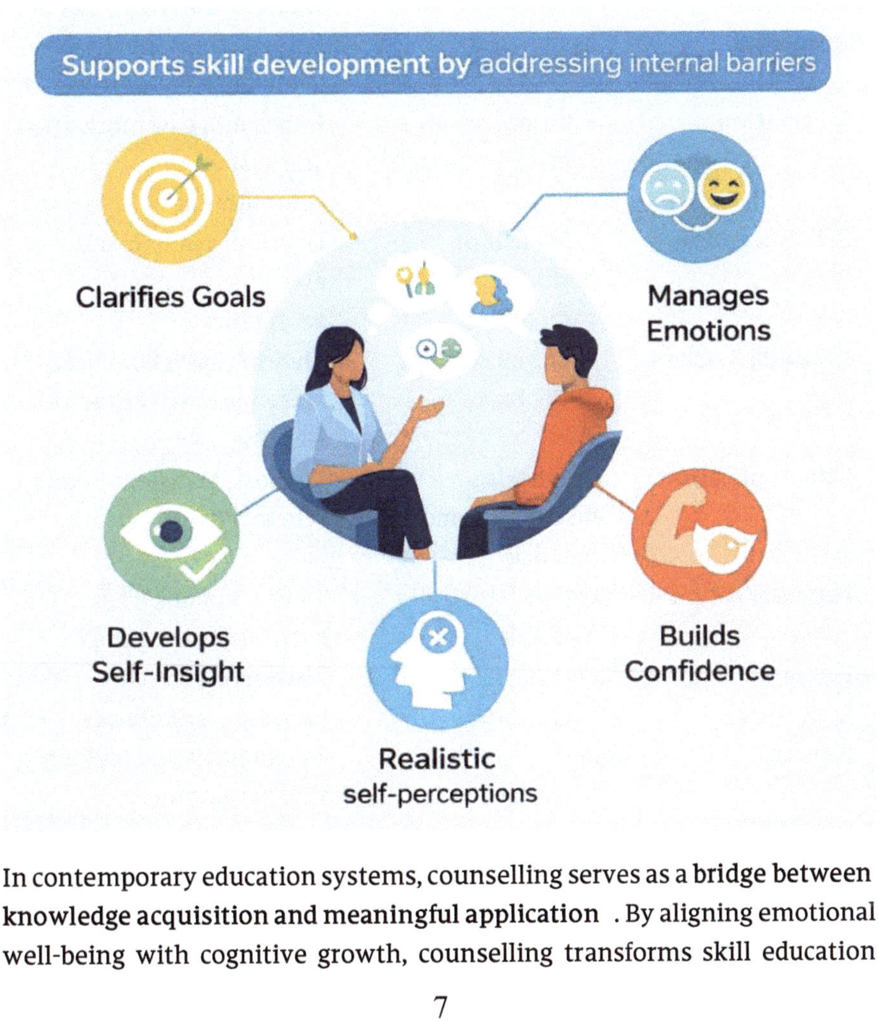

In contemporary education systems, counselling serves as a **bridge between knowledge acquisition and meaningful application** . By aligning emotional well-being with cognitive growth, counselling transforms skill education into a holistic developmental journey that prepares individuals for sustained success in academic, professional, and social contexts.

Aspect of Skill Development	Traditional Instruction Focus	Counselling Contribution
Goal Setting	Preset academic or training objectives	Helps learners clarify personal goals aligned with strengths and interests
Emotional Readiness	Largely ignored or assumed	Addresses anxiety, fear of failure, stress, and low confidence
Motivation	External rewards such as grades or certification	Builds intrinsic motivation and sustained commitment
Self-Perception	Emphasis on performance comparison	Develops realistic self-awareness and self-acceptance
Learning Barriers	Focus on content difficulty	Identifies psychological and emotional obstacles to learning
Skill Application	Emphasis on instruction and practice	Supports transfer of skills into real-life situations
Personalization	Uniform teaching methods	Tailors' guidance based on individual needs and learning styles
Long-Term Growth	Short-term performance outcomes	Encourages resilience, adaptability, and lifelong skill development

Multiple Choice Questions (MCQs)

1. Skill development in modern psychology is best described as:

a) A fixed trait determined at birth
b) A one-time learning activity
c) A dynamic process shaped by learning and experience
d) Limited only to vocational training

Answer: c) A dynamic process shaped by learning and experience

2. Which of the following best distinguishes psychological skills from technical skills?

a) Psychological skills are easier to measure
b) Technical skills focus on internal regulation and motivation
c) Psychological skills influence learning, adaptability, and performance
d) Technical skills determine long-term effectiveness

Answer: c) Psychological skills influence learning, adaptability, and performance

3. Skill development is considered a cognitive-emotional process because:

a) It depends only on intelligence
b) Emotions have no role in learning
c) Learning involves understanding concepts and managing emotions
d) Practice alone ensures mastery

Answer: c) Learning involves understanding concepts and managing emotions

4. Which psychological factor most strongly influences persistence during skill learning?

a) Age
b) Self-efficacy

c) Physical strength
d) Social status

Answer: b) Self-efficacy

5. The primary role of counselling in modern skill education is to:

a) Replace classroom instruction
b) Focus only on academic assessment
c) Address internal barriers and personalize skill development
d) Teach technical procedures directly

Answer: c) Address internal barriers and personalize skill development

Short Answer Questions

1. What is meant by skill development in psychological terms?
2. Differentiate between psychological skills and technical skills.
3. Why are skills considered dynamic rather than fixed traits?
4. How do emotions influence the process of skill acquisition?
5. What role does self-efficacy play in learning new skills?
6. How does counselling support effective skill development in modern education?

Long Answer Questions

1. Explain the meaning and evolution of skill development from a psychological perspective.
2. Discuss the differences between psychological skills and technical skills, highlighting their roles in long-term performance.

3. Describe skill development as an integrated cognitive and emotional process with suitable examples.
4. Examine the influence of beliefs, mindset, and emotional regulation on skill learning.
5. Analyse the role of counselling in transforming traditional skill education into a personalized growth process.

2

Understanding the Student Mind

2.1 Cognitive Development and Learning Capacity

Cognitive development influences how students process information, solve problems, and transfer knowledge across contexts. Attention span, memory capacity, reasoning ability, and processing speed vary significantly among learners.

Cognitive development shapes the way learners perceive, interpret, and apply information across academic and real-life situations. It encompasses mental processes such as attention, memory, reasoning, language comprehension, and problem-solving. These processes do not develop uniformly in all individuals. Students differ widely in their ability to concentrate for extended periods, retain and retrieve information, analyse abstract ideas, and respond quickly to new stimuli. Such variation is natural and reflects differences in neurological maturation, prior experiences, emotional states, and learning environments.

From a psychological perspective, learning is not a passive act of receiving information. Instead, cognition grows through active engagement with tasks, social interaction, and repeated practice. Learners build new understanding by connecting fresh information to existing knowledge structures. When content is presented without considering a learner's cognitive readiness, it can lead to overload, confusion, or disengagement. Conversely, when instruction aligns with the learner's developmental stage, it enhances comprehension and long-term retention.

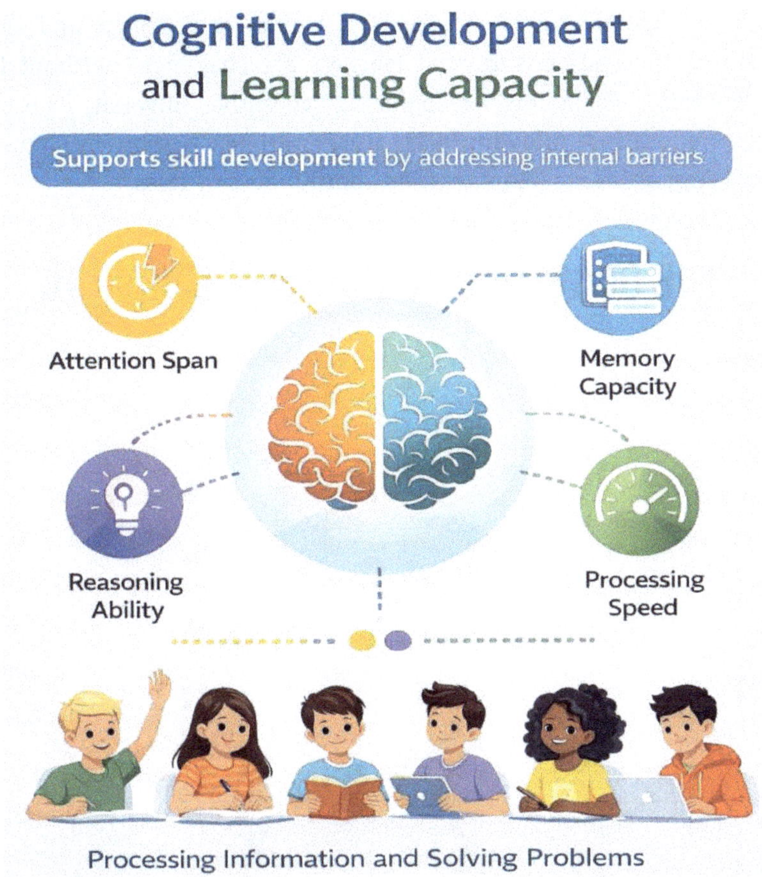

The concept of scaffolding is central to understanding learning capacity. Scaffolding involves providing temporary support-such as guided questions, examples, or visual aids-that helps learners perform tasks slightly beyond their current ability. As competence increases, these supports are gradually withdrawn, fostering independence and confidence. This approach recognizes that cognitive abilities evolve through guided effort rather than sudden mastery.

For educators and counsellors, understanding cognitive development enables the design of flexible learning strategies that respect individual differences. Differentiated instruction, adaptive pacing, and varied assessment methods ensure that learners are challenged without being overwhelmed. Ultimately, recognizing cognitive diversity promotes inclusive education, allowing each learner to reach their full potential through supportive, developmentally appropriate practices.

Example: Applying Cognitive Development in a Classroom Setting

Consider a middle-school classroom where students are learning to solve word-based mathematics problems. The teacher observes that while some students can quickly interpret the problem and apply formulas, others struggle to understand the language and sequence of steps involved. These differences reflect variations in attention span, working memory, and reasoning ability rather than a lack of intelligence.

To support cognitive development, the teacher uses **scaffolding strategies** . First, complex problems are broken into smaller, manageable steps. Visual aids such as diagrams and flowcharts are introduced to help students organize information. The teacher models problem-solving aloud, explaining the reasoning process step by step so learners can follow how decisions are made.

Students who need additional support are encouraged to work in pairs, allowing peer interaction to reinforce understanding. As learners gain confidence, the teacher gradually reduces guidance, asking students to attempt similar problems independently. Over time, students who initially required assistance become more capable of processing information, reasoning through steps, and transferring the strategy to new problems.

This example demonstrates how recognizing differences in cognitive development allows educators to adapt instruction. By aligning teaching methods with learners' cognitive capacities, educators promote deeper understanding, reduce frustration, and help students build lasting critical thinking skills.

2.2 Emotional Development and Academic Behaviour

Emotional maturity affects motivation, persistence, stress tolerance, and classroom behaviour. Students who struggle with emotional regulation often face difficulties in concentration and performance despite intellectual capability.

Emotional development plays a vital role in shaping students' academic behaviour and overall learning outcomes. It influences how learners respond to challenges, manage stress, sustain motivation, and interact within classroom environments. Emotional maturity enables students to regulate their feelings, remain focused during tasks, and persist even when learning becomes demanding. In contrast, learners who experience difficulty in emotional regulation may struggle with anxiety, frustration, or impulsive reactions, which can interfere with attention and academic performance despite having strong intellectual abilities.

Motivation is intricately linked to emotional well-being. Students who feel confident, supported, and emotionally secure are more likely to take initiative in learning and remain engaged over time. Emotional awareness helps learners recognize feelings such as fear of failure or test anxiety and respond to them in healthy ways rather than avoiding tasks or disengaging. It also allows students to accept feedback constructively, viewing mistakes as opportunities for growth instead of personal failures.

Stress tolerance is another key aspect of emotional development. Academic settings often involve deadlines, evaluations, and social expectations that can create pressure. Emotionally developed learners are better equipped to cope with such stress, maintain balance, and recover from setbacks. This resilience supports consistent effort and long-term academic success.

Counselling interventions play an important role in fostering emotional development. Through guided reflection, emotional skills training, and supportive dialogue, counselling helps students build self-awareness, regulate emotions, and develop coping strategies. As emotional competence improves, students are able to participate more actively in learning, collaborate effectively with peers, and acquire skills in a focused and confident manner.

Case Study: Emotional Development and Academic Behaviour

A case study from a senior secondary school highlights the impact of emotional development on academic behaviour. *Riya* (pseudonym), a Class XI student, demonstrated high intellectual ability and consistently scored well in internal assessments. However, during examinations and oral presentations, her performance declined sharply. Teachers observed frequent absenteeism on test days, visible anxiety, and difficulty concentrating in class discussions.

A counselling assessment revealed that Riya experienced intense fear of failure and struggled with emotional regulation under pressure. Minor setbacks, such as receiving average marks or critical feedback, triggered feelings of self-doubt and withdrawal. Although she understood the subject content, her emotional responses interfered with sustained effort and performance.

A structured counselling intervention was introduced over eight weeks. The counsellor focused on emotional awareness, helping Riya identify anxiety triggers and physical stress responses. Techniques such as guided breathing, cognitive reframing, and goal-setting were practiced regularly. Teachers collaborated by providing formative feedback and low-stakes assessments to rebuild confidence.

Gradually, Riya's classroom behaviour improved. She began participating actively, showed greater persistence in challenging tasks, and approached examinations with reduced anxiety. By the end of the term, her academic performance aligned more closely with her intellectual potential.

This case study illustrates how emotional development directly influences academic behaviour. With appropriate counselling support, students can strengthen emotional regulation, improve engagement, and achieve more consistent learning outcomes.

2.3 Social Development and Peer Influence

Students develop within social environments shaped by peer interaction, family expectations, and cultural norms. Social development influences communication skills, teamwork, leadership, and adaptability. Peer validation can enhance confidence or contribute to self-doubt, depending on context.

Social development refers to the gradual ability of students to interact effectively with others and to understand social roles, expectations, and norms. Learning does not occur in isolation; it is deeply embedded within social environments shaped by peer relationships, family influences, school culture, and broader societal values. These environments significantly affect how students communicate, cooperate, and perceive themselves within academic and social settings.

Peer interaction plays a particularly powerful role during childhood and adolescence. Through group activities, discussions, and informal interactions, students develop communication skills, empathy, conflict resolution abilities, and teamwork. Positive peer relationships can boost confidence, motivation, and a sense of belonging, encouraging active participation in learning. Conversely, negative peer experiences-such as exclusion, comparison, or ridicule-may lead to self-doubt, withdrawal, or reduced academic engagement, even among capable learners.

Social development also shapes leadership and adaptability. Students who are socially confident are more likely to take initiative, collaborate effectively, and adjust to diverse viewpoints. Exposure to varied social contexts helps learners become flexible and culturally sensitive, skills that are increasingly important in modern educational and professional environments.

For counsellors and educators, understanding social dynamics is essential. By recognizing peer influence patterns and social pressures, they can guide students toward healthy collaboration, constructive peer relationships, and positive interpersonal growth. Counselling interventions, group activities, and inclusive classroom practices help students build social competence, manage peer influence responsibly, and develop a strong, balanced sense of self within their learning communities.

2.4 Psychological Diversity Among Learners

No two learners share identical psychological profiles. Differences in temperament, emotional sensitivity, learning pace, and motivation create diverse learning needs. Recognizing psychological diversity prevents unfair comparisons and labelling.

Psychological diversity recognizes that every learner brings a unique combination of cognitive, emotional, and behavioural characteristics into the learning environment. No two students process information, respond to challenges, or stay motivated in exactly the same way. Variations in temperament, emotional sensitivity, attention span, learning pace, confidence levels, and intrinsic motivation shape how individuals engage with academic tasks and social interactions.

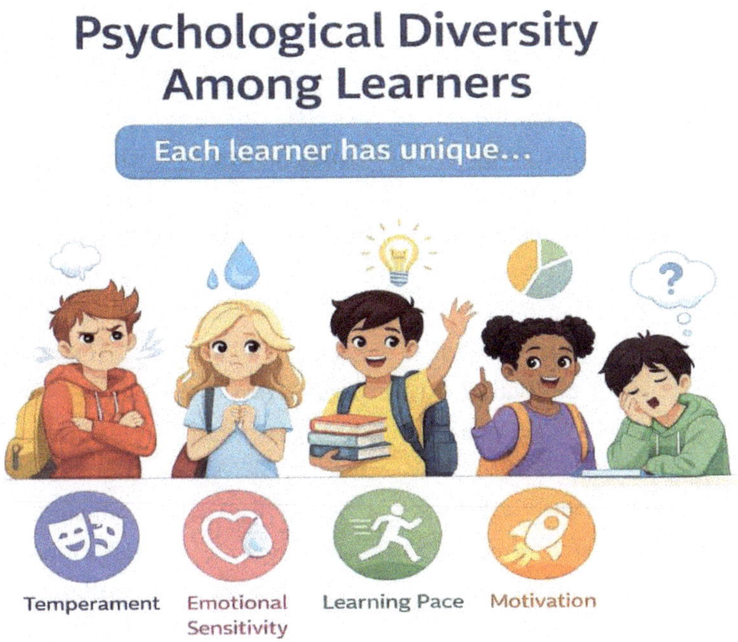

When these differences are ignored, students are often subjected to unfair comparisons and rigid expectations. Labelling learners as “slow,” “weak,” or “problematic” can negatively affect self-esteem and long-term motivation, even when the learner possesses strong potential in other areas. Psychological research emphasizes that such labels do not reflect fixed ability but rather temporary mismatches between teaching approaches and individual learner needs.

Psychological Dimension	Common Learner Differences	Possible Learning Challenges	Counselling-Centric Support Strategies
Temperament	Introverted, extroverted, emotionally sensitive, emotionally stable	Fear of participation, impulsive behaviour, social withdrawal	Individual counselling, confidence-building activities, structured peer interaction
Learning Pace	Adaptive people, average learners, reflective or slow-paced learners	Anxiety due to time pressure, incomplete understanding	Flexible timelines, personalized study plans, reinforcement sessions
Motivation Style	Intrinsically motivated, extrinsically motivated, low motivation	Lack of persistence, disengagement from tasks	Goal-setting, values clarification, motivational counselling
Emotional Sensitivity	Extremely sensitive, moderately responsive, emotionally resilient	Stress, test anxiety, fear of failure	Emotional regulation training, stress-management techniques

Attention & Focus	Sustained attention, fluctuating focus, distractibility	Difficulty completing tasks, inconsistent performance	Attention-training exercises, structured routines, behavioural strategies
Self-Concept & Confidence	High self-confidence, self-doubt, perfectionism	Avoidance of challenges, fear of feedback	Self-reflection sessions, positive reinforcement, growth-mindset counselling

A counselling-centric educational approach places psychological diversity at the centre of learning design. Instead of enforcing uniform methods, it helps students identify their personal strengths-such as creativity, analytical thinking, empathy, or perseverance-while also acknowledging areas that require support. Counsellors work with learners to develop compensatory strategies, such as time-management techniques, emotional regulation skills, alternative study methods, or social support systems.

This inclusive perspective encourages self-acceptance and resilience. When students understand that diversity in psychological makeup is normal and valuable, they are more likely to engage positively with learning. Over time, this approach promotes sustainable skill development, emotional well-being, and a balanced sense of competence, allowing learners to progress at their own pace while building confidence and lifelong learning habits.

2.5 Learning Styles and Intelligence Theories

Learning styles and intelligence theories explain how students differ in processing information and expressing abilities, highlighting that learning is not uniform. Understanding these differences helps educators

and counsellors personalize instruction, build confidence, and unlock each learner's unique potential.

Understanding how students learn requires attention to both **learning styles** and **intelligence theories** , as these frameworks explain why learners differ in their approaches to acquiring, processing, and applying knowledge. Traditional education often assumes a uniform learning pattern, but psychology demonstrates that students vary widely in how they perceive information, engage with content, and demonstrate understanding. Recognizing these differences is essential for effective teaching, counselling, and learner-centred education.

Learning styles refer to preferred ways individuals absorb and process information. Some students learn best through **visual methods**, such as diagrams, charts, and written notes, while others rely more on **auditory input**, benefiting from discussions, lectures, and verbal explanations. **Kinaesthetic learners** understand concepts more effectively through firsthand activities, movement, and practical application. These preferences are not rigid categories but tendencies that shape engagement and comprehension. When teaching methods align with a student's dominant learning style, attention improves, anxiety decreases, and learning becomes more meaningful. Counselling helps students identify their learning preferences, reducing self-blame when traditional methods feel ineffective and encouraging adaptive strategies rather than withdrawal.

Intelligence theories expand this understanding by challenging the idea that intelligence is a single, fixed ability measured only by exams or IQ scores. Classical views emphasized logical and linguistic abilities, but modern psychology highlights intelligence as **multidimensional and dynamic** . One influential perspective is the theory of multiple intelligences, which proposes that individuals possess different combinations of intellectual strengths-such as linguistic, logical, spatial, interpersonal, intrapersonal, and bodily intelligence. From this view, a student struggling with written tests may excel in social understanding, creativity, or practical problem-solving. These reframing shifts education from ranking students to recognizing potential.

Another key contribution comes from theories distinguishing **fluid intelligence** (problem-solving and reasoning ability) and **crystallized intelligence** (knowledge gained through experience and learning). Fluid intelligence supports adaptability and novel thinking, while crystallized intelligence grows with education and exposure. Counselling plays a crucial role in helping students understand that intelligence can develop over time, especially through effort, strategy, and supportive environments.

Integrating learning styles with intelligence theories creates a holistic picture of the student mind. It explains why one-size-fits-all instruction limits growth and why emotional responses-such as frustration, boredom, or confidence-are closely tied to learning experiences. Counselling-centred education uses these frameworks to personalize learning pathways, validate diverse abilities, and build self-efficacy. Ultimately, understanding learning styles and intelligence theories empowers students to learn *how* they learn, transforming education from passive instruction into active psychological development.

Multiple Choice Questions (MCQs)

1. Which factor most directly influences how students process and retain new information?

a) Classroom size

b) Cognitive development level

c) School infrastructure

d) Examination pattern

Answer: b) Cognitive development level

2. Emotional regulation primarily helps students to:

a) Memorize content faster

b) Avoid peer interaction

c) Manage stress and respond constructively to challenges

d) Eliminate academic competition

Answer: c) Manage stress and respond constructively to challenges

3. **Peer influence in learning environments can best be described as:**

a) Always harmful to academic performance

b) Irrelevant to individual learning

c) Capable of enhancing or reducing confidence depending on context

d) Limited only to extracurricular activities

Answer: c) Capable of enhancing or reducing confidence depending on context

4. **Psychological diversity among learners suggests that:**

a) All students should be taught using identical methods

b) Intelligence is fixed and uniform

c) Learners differ in temperament, motivation, and learning pace

d) Comparison improves student performance

Answer: c) Learners differ in temperament, motivation, and learning pace

5. **A counselling-centric educational approach primarily aims to:**

a) Replace classroom teaching

b) Label students based on ability

c) Support emotional well-being and individualized learning growth

d) Focus only on academic achievement

Answer: c) Support emotional well-being and individualized learning growth

Short Answer Questions

1. Define cognitive development and explain its role in student learning.
2. How does emotional regulation influence academic performance?
3. What is meant by peer influence in the context of student development?
4. List any two factors that contribute to psychological diversity among learners.
5. Why is scaffolding important in supporting students' learning capacity?
6. How does counselling help students manage academic stress?

Long Answer Questions

1. Discuss the relationship between cognitive development and learning capacity, highlighting the role of attention, memory, and reasoning.
2. Explain how emotional development affects motivation, persistence, and classroom behaviour, with suitable examples.
3. Analyse the impact of social development and peer influence on students' confidence and academic engagement.

4. Describe psychological diversity among learners and explain why recognizing it is essential for inclusive education.

5. Examine the role of counselling-centric education in supporting students with varied emotional and learning needs.

3

Motivation and Skill Acquisition

3.1 Intrinsic and Extrinsic Motivation

Motivation drives the willingness to engage in sustained practice. Intrinsic motivation arises from internal interest, curiosity, and personal satisfaction, while extrinsic motivation depends on rewards, grades, or social approval. Psychology shows that intrinsic motivation leads to deeper learning and long-term skill retention.

Motivation is the psychological force that determines why and how consistently a student engages in learning activities. It directly influences attention, persistence, and the quality of effort invested in academic tasks.

Broadly, motivation operates in two interconnected forms: **intrinsic** and **extrinsic** motivation.

Intrinsic motivation originates from within the learner. It is driven by genuine interest, curiosity, enjoyment, or a sense of personal meaning. When students are intrinsically motivated, they learn because the activity itself feels rewarding. For example, a student who reads beyond the syllabus out of curiosity or practices a skill to master it experiences satisfaction from the learning process. Psychological research consistently shows that intrinsic motivation supports deeper cognitive processing, creativity, conceptual understanding, and long-term retention of knowledge. Learners motivated from within are more likely to persist even in the face of difficulty.

Extrinsic motivation, in contrast, is influenced by external factors such as grades, certificates, praise, competition, or social recognition. While extrinsic incentives can be effective in initiating engagement-especially when interest is low-they often encourage short-term compliance rather than sustained learning. Overreliance on rewards may lead students to focus on outcomes rather than understanding, reducing autonomy and internal drive over time.

Counsellors and educators play a critical role in **shifting students from reward-dependent behaviour to purpose-driven engagement** . This transition is supported by helping learners identify personal goals, connect academic tasks to real-life relevance, and reflect on their strengths and interests. By fostering autonomy, competence, and a sense of purpose, counselling interventions help students internalize motivation-transforming learning from an obligation into a meaningful personal journey.

3.2 Goal-Setting Psychology in Skill Development

Effective goals provide direction, structure, and measurable progress. Psychological research highlights that clear, realistic, and personally meaningful goals enhance persistence. Short-term goals support daily practice, while long-term goals provide vision and identity.

Goal-setting is a foundational psychological mechanism that shapes how individuals acquire and refine skills over time. Well-defined goals act as a **cognitive roadmap**, giving learners clarity about what they are working toward, how progress can be measured, and why sustained effort is worthwhile. Without clear goals, practice often becomes inconsistent and directionless, limiting skill growth.

Psychological research shows that **effective goals are specific, realistic, and personally meaningful**. Vague intentions such as "do better" or "practice more" fail to guide behaviour, whereas clear goals-like improving a particular skill within a set timeframe-focus attention and regulate effort. When goals are attainable yet challenging, they enhance persistence by creating a balance between effort and confidence. Achieving such goals also reinforces self-efficacy, motivating learners to continue improving.

Goal-setting works best when it operates at **multiple levels**. Short-term goals support daily or weekly practice by breaking complex skills into manageable steps. They provide frequent feedback and a sense of accomplishment, which sustains motivation during routine effort. Long-term goals, on the other hand, offer a broader vision. They help learners connect present practice to future aspirations, shaping identity and purpose-for example, seeing oneself as a competent professional, artist, or researcher.

Counselling plays a crucial role in helping students **align goals with their abilities, values, and life aspirations** . Through guided reflection, counsellors help learners set realistic expectations, prioritize goals, and adjust them when circumstances change. This process prevents burnout caused by unrealistic demands and reduces discouragement arising from repeated failure. By grounding goals in personal meaning and psychological readiness, counselling transforms goal-setting into a sustainable framework for long-term skill development.

Example: Goal-Setting Psychology in Skill Development

Consider a college student learning **public speaking** .

Long-term goal (vision and identity):
The student aims to become a confident communicator capable of delivering professional presentations and participating effectively in seminars. This long-term goal shapes the student's identity as a capable speaker and provides a clear sense of purpose.

Short-term goals (daily practice):
To reach this vision, the student sets small, achievable goals such as:

- Practicing a 3-minute speech in front of a mirror twice a week
- Recording one practice speech every weekend
- Improving eye contact and voice clarity in each session

These short-term goals make practice structured and measurable, preventing overwhelm.

Role of counselling:
A counsellor helps the student assess current abilities and manage anxiety related to speaking in public. Together, they adjust goals to remain realistic-for example, starting with speaking in small groups before addressing larger audiences. The counsellor also links the goal to the student's career aspirations, reinforcing its personal relevance.

Outcome:
Because the goals are aligned with the student's skills, values, and future ambitions, the student remains motivated, avoids burnout, and gradually develops confidence and competence in public speaking through consistent, focused effort.

3.3 Motivation Barriers in Students

Many students experience motivational decline due to fear of failure, comparison, unclear purpose, or past negative experiences. These barriers often manifest as procrastination or disengagement rather than lack of ability. Psychology emphasizes that motivation fluctuates and can be rebuilt through supportive intervention.

Motivational barriers are common in students and often misunderstood as laziness or lack of capability. In reality, these barriers usually stem from emotional, cognitive, or environmental factors that interfere with a student's willingness to engage consistently in learning or skill development. Understanding these barriers is essential for effective academic and personal growth.

One major barrier is the fear of failure. Students who associate mistakes with embarrassment, punishment, or loss of self-worth may avoid tasks altogether to protect their self-esteem. Similarly, constant comparison with peers can weaken motivation, especially when students perceive themselves as falling behind. Instead of inspiring improvement, comparison may create anxiety, self-doubt, and withdrawal from effort.

Another significant obstacle is an **unclear sense of purpose** . When students do not understand why they are learning a particular skill or how it connects to their future, effort feels meaningless. Past **negative academic experiences**, such as repeated criticism, poor grades, or discouraging feedback, can further reinforce avoidance patterns. Over time, these experiences shape beliefs like "I'm not good at this" or "trying won't help," which suppress motivation.

These barriers rarely appear as open resistance. More often, they manifest as **procrastination, inconsistency, distraction, or emotional disengagement** . Psychology recognizes that motivation is not a fixed trait; it naturally fluctuates and can be restored under the right conditions. Supportive environments, positive feedback, and gradual success experiences help rebuild confidence and interest.

Counselling plays a critical role by **identifying emotional triggers and unhelpful thought patterns** that block motivation. Through dialogue and reflection, counsellors help students reframe failure, set realistic expectations, and reconnect effort with personal meaning. By addressing the underlying psychological blocks rather than surface behaviours, counselling enables students to re-engage with learning and continue skill development in a healthier, more sustainable way.

Example: Motivation Barriers in Students

Consider a high school student struggling with **mathematics**.

Motivation barrier:
The student previously performed poorly on a few math tests and received negative feedback in class. Over time, this led to a fear of failure and the belief that "I am not good at math." The student begins comparing themselves with classmates who solve problems quickly, which further lowers confidence. As a result, the student avoids homework, delays studying, and appears disengaged during lessons.

How the barrier manifests:
Rather than lacking ability, the student shows signs of procrastination and anxiety. They hesitate to ask questions, rush through assignments, or skip practice altogether to avoid the possibility of making mistakes.

Role of counselling:
A counsellor helps the student identify the emotional impact of past failures and challenges the fixed belief about intelligence. Together, they reframe mistakes as part of learning and set small, manageable goals-such as mastering one concept at a time. The counsellor also reduces peer comparison by focusing on individual progress rather than class rankings.

Outcome:
With emotional support and clearer expectations, the student gradually regains confidence. Motivation improves as effort leads to small successes, demonstrating that the barrier was psychological rather than a lack of ability.

3.4 Counselling Techniques to Enhance Motivation

Counselling enhances motivation through reflective dialogue, cognitive restructuring, and encouragement of self-efficacy. Techniques such as positive self-talk, progress tracking, value clarification, and feedback interpretation help students regain momentum.

Counselling plays a vital role in strengthening and sustaining student motivation, especially during long and demanding skill-development journeys. Rather than relying on external pressure or rewards, counselling focuses on **internal psychological processes** that influence effort, persistence, and self-belief.

One key technique is **reflective dialogue**, where counsellors create a safe space for students to express doubts, frustrations, and fears without judgment. Through guided questioning, students gain insight into their own thought patterns and emotional responses, helping them understand why motivation may be declining. This awareness is the first step toward meaningful change.

Cognitive restructuring is another essential approach. Students often carry unhelpful beliefs such as "I will never improve" or "Others are naturally better than me." Counsellors help challenge and reframe these thoughts into realistic, growth-oriented perspectives. This shift reduces anxiety and prevents negative self-talk from undermining effort.

Counselling also emphasizes building **self-efficacy**, or the belief in one's ability to succeed through effort. Techniques such as positive self-talk, recognition of small achievements, and **progress tracking** help students see evidence of improvement. When learners observe consistent progress, motivation becomes self-sustaining.

Additional strategies include **value clarification**, which helps students connect skills to personal goals and life meaning, and **feedback interpretation**, where counsellors guide students to view feedback as information for growth rather than judgment. By reinforcing effort, learning, and persistence over immediate outcomes, counselling transforms fragile motivation into a **stable psychological foundation**, enabling long-term engagement and effective skill acquisition.

3.5 Role of Counsellors in Lifelong Skill Development

Counsellors act as long-term facilitators of growth rather than one-time advisors. They help students plan skill pathways, reflect on learning experiences, and navigate career changes across the lifespan. Through mentoring, goal review, and emotional support, counselling ensures that learning remains purposeful, sustainable, and aligned with evolving personal and professional goals.

In contemporary education and career landscapes, counsellors play a pivotal role not merely as short-term analytical people but as long-term partners in personal and professional growth. Lifelong skill development requires continuous reflection, adaptation, and decision-making, all of which benefit from structured psychological support. Counsellors help individuals understand that learning is not confined to formal education but extends across different life stages, career transitions, and personal transformations.

Section	Key Focus	Core Psychological Insight	Role of Counselling
3.1 Intrinsic and Extrinsic Motivation	Sources of motivation	Intrinsic motivation (interest, curiosity, satisfaction) leads to deeper learning and	Helps students shift from reward-driven behaviour to

		long-term retention, while extrinsic motivation (grades, rewards, approval) supports short-term engagement	purpose-driven engagement
3.2 Goal-Setting Psychology	Structure and direction of effort	Clear, realistic, and meaningful goals enhance persistence; short-term goals support daily practice, long-term goals provide vision and identity	Assists students in aligning goals with abilities, values, and life aspirations
3.3 Motivation Barriers in Students	Obstacles to engagement	Fear of failure, comparison, unclear purpose, and past negative experiences reduce motivation; barriers appear as procrastination or disengagement	Identifies emotional and cognitive blocks underlying motivational decline
3.4 Counselling Techniques to Enhance Motivation	Psychological intervention methods	Motivation strengthens through self-efficacy, reflection, and cognitive reframing rather than pressure or rewards	Uses reflective dialogue, cognitive restructuring, progress tracking, and value clarification

Multiple Choice Questions (MCQs)

1. Which type of motivation is most strongly associated with deep learning and long-term skill retention?

A. Extrinsic motivation
B. Social motivation
C. Intrinsic motivation
D. Competitive motivation

Correct Answer: C. Intrinsic motivation

2. Extrinsic motivation primarily relies on which of the following factors?

A. Personal curiosity and interest
B. Internal satisfaction and enjoyment
C. Rewards, grades, or social approval
D. Self-reflection and autonomy

Correct Answer: C. Rewards, grades, or social approval

3. Why are short-term goals important in skill development?

A. They replace long-term goals
B. They reduce the need for effort
C. They support daily practice and measurable progress
D. They eliminate the risk of failure

Correct Answer: C. They support daily practice and measurable progress

4. Motivation barriers in students most commonly appear as:

A. Lack of intelligence
B. Laziness and indiscipline
C. Procrastination and disengagement
D. Absence of learning resources

Correct Answer: C. Procrastination and disengagement

5. Which counselling approach helps students challenge negative beliefs and rebuild confidence?

A. External reward reinforcement
B. Cognitive restructuring
C. Competitive comparison
D. Outcome-based evaluation

Correct Answer: B. Cognitive restructuring

Short Answer Questions

1. Define intrinsic motivation and explain its role in long-term skill development.
2. Distinguish between intrinsic and extrinsic motivation with one example each.
3. Why are short-term goals important in sustaining daily practice?
4. List any two common motivation barriers faced by students.
5. How does fear of failure affect student motivation?
6. What is meant by self-efficacy in the context of skill acquisition?

Long Answer Questions

1. Explain the concepts of intrinsic and extrinsic motivation and analyse their impact on learning and skill retention.
2. Discuss the psychological importance of goal-setting in skill development, highlighting the role of short-term and long-term goals.
3. Examine the major motivational barriers experienced by students and explain how they influence learning behaviour.

4. Describe the role of counselling in identifying and addressing emotional and cognitive blocks to motivation.

5. Evaluate various counselling techniques used to enhance student motivation and persistence in learning.

4

Self-Awareness and Skill Identity

4.1 Understanding Self-Awareness in Skill Development

Self-awareness refers to an individual's ability to recognize their own abilities, limitations, interests, values, and emotional patterns. In the context of skill development, self-awareness acts as the foundation upon which effective learning and career decisions are built.

Self-awareness is a critical internal capacity that enables individuals to understand who they are as learners and future professionals. It involves a conscious recognition of one's strengths, weaknesses, interests, values, attitudes, and emotional responses. In the context of skill development, self-awareness functions as the starting point for meaningful learning, because skills acquired without self-understanding often remain underutilized or misaligned with personal goals.

When students are self-aware, they are better able to identify how they learn best-whether through practice, observation, collaboration, or reflection. This understanding allows them to adopt learning strategies that suit their cognitive style, leading to improved skill acquisition and retention. For example, a learner who recognizes difficulty with time management can consciously work on organizational skills alongside technical competencies, creating a more balanced development process.

Self-awareness also supports informed career and skill-pathway decisions. Students who understand their interests and values are less likely to follow trends blindly and more likely to pursue skills that align with their long-term aspirations. This alignment increases motivation, persistence, and satisfaction, which are essential for mastering complex or evolving skills in a competitive environment.

From a psychological perspective, self-awareness is not an inborn trait but a developmental process. It grows through regular self-reflection, constructive feedback from teachers and peers, and guided experiences such as mentoring, counselling, and experiential learning. Educational environments that encourage reflection, goal-setting, and open dialogue play a crucial role in nurturing self-awareness. Ultimately, self-aware learners become initiative-taking, adaptable, and resilient-qualities that significantly enhance their ability to develop relevant and sustainable skills throughout life.

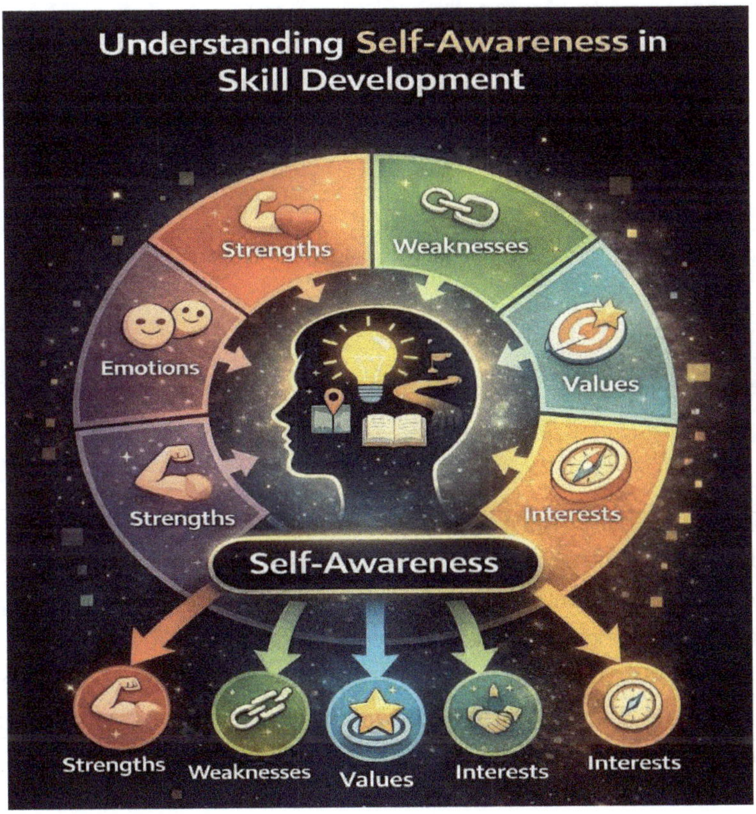

Example: Self-Awareness in Skill Development

Consider a college student pursuing a degree in computer science. During the initial semesters, the student performs well in theoretical subjects such as algorithms and data structures but consistently struggles in competitive coding and timed programming tests. Through self-reflection and feedback from instructors, the student becomes aware that while they have strong analytical thinking skills, they experience anxiety under time pressure and need more firsthand practice.

Recognizing this pattern, the student consciously adjusts their skill-development approach. Instead of focusing only on advanced coding challenges, they begin by strengthening fundamentals through small, daily programming tasks and collaborative projects. They also practice mock coding sessions to gradually become comfortable with time constraints. At the same time, the student realizes a strong interest in system design and problem analysis rather than fast-paced coding competitions.

As a result of this self-awareness, the student chooses to develop skills aligned with roles such as software architecture or data analysis, where deep thinking and structured problem-solving are valued. This alignment improves motivation, learning efficiency, and confidence. The example shows how self-awareness helps learners identify suitable skill pathways, adapt learning strategies, and make informed career decisions rather than following a one-size-fits-all approach.

4.2 Identifying Strengths, Weaknesses, and Interests

Skill identity emerges when students clearly identify what they are naturally inclined toward and where they require support. Strengths reflect areas of ease and confidence, while weaknesses indicate opportunities for structured improvement rather than failure. Interests sustain long-term engagement and persistence.

Identifying strengths, weaknesses, and interests is a vital step in shaping a student's skill identity. Skill identity refers to a clear understanding of one's natural inclinations, learned abilities, and areas that need development. When students are able to recognize these elements honestly, they gain clarity about how to channel their efforts effectively rather than relying on trial and error.

Strengths represent areas where students experience confidence, ease, and consistent performance. These may emerge in academic subjects, creative activities, communication, leadership, or problem-solving. Recognizing strengths allows learners to build competence and self-esteem, as skills developed in these areas often progress more quickly and with greater motivation. At the same time, weaknesses should not be viewed as signs of inadequacy. Instead, they indicate domains that require structured support, alternative strategies, or additional time for improvement.

Interests play a crucial role in sustaining long-term engagement. Even when a task is challenging, genuine interest encourages persistence and resilience. Students are more likely to invest effort in skill development when the activity aligns with what they find meaningful or enjoyable. Interests often reveal themselves through voluntary participation, curiosity, and emotional satisfaction rather than formal assessments alone.

Counselling and guided reflection help students make sense of these patterns. By analysing academic performance, participation in extracurricular activities, and emotional reactions to different tasks, students can develop a realistic and empowering self-profile. This process supports informed decision-making, reduces anxiety caused by unrealistic expectations, and enables learners to pursue skill pathways that align with both their capabilities and aspirations.

Case Study: Identifying Strengths, Weaknesses, and Interests in Skill Development

Riya, a first-year undergraduate student, enrolled in a general science program with no clear understanding of her skill strengths or career direction. During her first semester, her academic performance showed an interesting pattern. She scored highly in subjects that required presentations, group discussions, and written explanations but struggled in subjects involving numerical problem-solving and timed examinations. Outside the classroom, she actively participated in debates, student clubs, and event coordination, displaying enthusiasm and confidence in collaborative environments.

Through academic counselling sessions, Riya was encouraged to reflect on her experiences rather than focusing only on grades. By reviewing her coursework, extracurricular involvement, and emotional responses to different activities, she identified her strengths in communication, organization, and leadership. Her weaknesses in quantitative subjects were reframed not as failure but as areas requiring additional academic support and alternative learning methods.

Further reflection revealed a strong interest in social engagement and advocacy-related activities. With guidance from the counsellor, Riya decided to develop skills aligned with fields such as public relations, social research, or education rather than forcing herself into a purely technical pathway. She enrolled in workshops on communication skills, leadership training, and research writing while seeking tutoring support for essential quantitative courses.

This case demonstrates how identifying strengths, weaknesses, and interests helps students develop a realistic skill identity. With counselling support, learners can make informed decisions that enhance confidence, sustain motivation, and promote long-term academic and professional growth.

4.3 Career Personality Theories

Career personality theories explain how individual traits, preferences, and behavioural tendencies influence occupational suitability. Students often struggle when their chosen paths conflict with their psychological makeup. Understanding personality-skill alignment prevents dissatisfaction and underperformance. Counselling bridges this gap by helping learners connect personal traits with skill demands, ensuring that career preparation aligns with both aptitude and temperament.

Career personality refers to the unique combination of an individual's traits, preferences, values, and behavioural tendencies that shape how they approach work and learning. Career personality theories emphasize that people differ in how they interact with tasks, environments, and challenges. When students choose skill pathways or careers that align with their psychological makeup, they are more likely to experience satisfaction, confidence, and sustained performance.

Difficulties often arise when there is a mismatch between a student's personality and the demands of a chosen field. For example, a learner with a strong preference for structure and predictability may feel stressed in highly ambiguous or fast-changing roles, while someone who thrives on creativity and autonomy may feel constrained in rigid, rule-driven environments. Such misalignment can lead to frustration, loss of motivation, and underperformance, even when the individual is capable.

Understanding personality–skill alignment helps students make more realistic and fulfilling career decisions. It encourages them to assess not only what skills are required in a profession but also how those skills are applied in daily work settings. This awareness reduces the risk of burnout and dissatisfaction by ensuring that learning efforts are invested in roles that suit both aptitude and temperament.

Counselling plays a crucial role in bridging this gap. Through personality assessments, reflective discussions, and exposure to different career scenarios, counsellors help students connect personal traits with the skill demands of various occupations. This guided process enables learners to prepare for careers that align with who they are, not just what they can do, leading to more meaningful and sustainable professional development.

4.4 Counselling Tools for Self-Discovery

Structured counselling tools such as reflective journaling, guided questioning, aptitude exploration, and narrative exercises support self-discovery. These methods encourage students to articulate experiences, analyse patterns, and reframe self-doubt.

Self-discovery is a foundational process in effective skill development, and structured counselling tools play a vital role in making this process purposeful and actionable. Many students possess fragmented self-knowledge but struggle to articulate it clearly. Counselling tools help organize thoughts, experiences, and emotions into meaningful insights that support informed decision-making.

Reflective journaling is one of the most effective tools for self-discovery. By regularly writing about learning experiences, challenges, successes, and emotional responses, students begin to recognize recurring patterns in their behaviour and motivation. Over time, journaling helps them understand what energizes them, what causes stress, and how they respond to different learning environments.

Together, these counselling tools transform self-awareness from an abstract idea into a practical roadmap. They guide students in selecting appropriate skills, adopting effective learning strategies, and preparing for careers that align with their identity, strengths, and long-term goals.

Counselling Tool	Purpose	How It Supports Self-Discovery	Impact on Skill & Career Development
Reflective Journaling	Encourage self-reflection	Helps students record experiences, emotions, and learning outcomes to identify recurring patterns	Improves self-awareness, clarity in learning preferences, and informed skill selection

Guided Questioning	Deepen self-exploration	Prompts learners to examine beliefs, motivations, strengths, and challenges through structured dialogue	Supports realistic goal-setting and adaptive learning strategies
Aptitude Exploration	Identify natural abilities and potential	Assesses cognitive, technical, and interpersonal tendencies without comparison pressure	Aligns skill development with aptitude, reducing frustration and mismatch
Narrative Exercises	Reframe self-perception	Enables students to tell and reinterpret their personal learning and life stories	Builds confidence, resilience, and a coherent career identity
Feedback Mapping	Interpret external input	Helps students analyse feedback from teachers, peers, and mentors constructively	Converts feedback into actionable improvement plans
Goal Visualization	Clarify future direction	Encourages students to imagine preferred roles and skill applications	Enhances motivation and career readiness through clear direction

Guided questioning is another powerful method used in counselling sessions. Through carefully framed questions, counsellors prompt students to examine their assumptions, values, and choices. Questions such as "When do you feel most confident while learning?" or "What type of tasks do you avoid and why?" encourage deeper self-exploration beyond surface-level responses.

Aptitude exploration tools, including structured assessments and skill-mapping activities, help students identify areas of natural ability and developmental potential. These tools shift the focus from comparison with others to personal growth. Narrative exercises, where students tell their own learning or life stories, further support this process by helping them reframe self-doubt, recognize resilience, and identify turning points.

Multiple Choice Questions (MCQs)

1. Self-awareness in skill development primarily refers to a student's ability to:

a) Memorize academic content quickly
b) Recognize personal strengths, weaknesses, interests, and learning patterns
c) Compete effectively with peers
d) Follow prescribed career paths

Answer: b

2. Why is self-awareness considered the foundation of effective skill development?

a) It guarantees academic success
b) It eliminates the need for guidance
c) It helps learners choose suitable skills and learning strategies
d) It focuses only on strengths and ignores weaknesses

Answer: c

3. In the context of skill identity, weaknesses should be viewed as:

a) Indicators of failure
b) Permanent limitations

c) Areas requiring structured support and improvement
d) Reasons to avoid certain subjects entirely

Answer: c

4. Career personality and skill alignment help students by:

a) Encouraging them to follow popular career trends
b) Matching skills with psychological traits and temperament
c) Reducing the importance of interests
d) Focusing only on academic performance

Answer: b

5. Which of the following counselling tools best helps students recognize patterns in their learning and emotions over time?

a) Competitive testing
b) Reflective journaling
c) Rote practice
d) External comparison

Answer: b

Short Answer Questions

1. Define self-awareness in relation to skill development.
2. What is meant by skill identity?
3. How do strengths influence a student's learning choices?
4. Why are interests important for sustaining skill development?
5. What is career personality?
6. Name any one counselling tool used for self-discovery.

Long Answer Questions

1. Explain the role of self-awareness in shaping effective skill-development pathways.
2. Discuss how identifying strengths, weaknesses, and interests helps students build a realistic skill identity.
3. Describe career personality and explain why aligning skills with personality is important.
4. Analyse the role of counselling in bridging the gap between student traits and career demands.
5. Explain various counselling tools used for self-discovery and their significance in career readiness.
6. Evaluate how self-awareness contributes to long-term career satisfaction and adaptability.

5

Emotional Intelligence and Skill Development

5.1 Emotional Regulation and Self-Management

Emotional regulation refers to the ability to recognize, manage, and respond appropriately to one's emotions. Students who struggle to control frustration, anxiety, or impulsivity often find skill development overwhelming. Psychology highlights that emotional regulation enables focus, perseverance, and adaptability.

Emotional regulation and self-management are essential psychological skills that influence how students engage with learning, cope with challenges, and develop competencies over time. Emotional regulation refers to the capacity to identify one's emotional states, understand their causes, and consciously adjust emotional responses in a constructive manner. Self-management extends this ability into action, enabling students to organize their behaviour, sustain motivation, and persist toward goals despite internal or external pressures.

Students who experience difficulty managing emotions such as frustration, fear of failure, anxiety, or impulsivity often find skill acquisition demanding. Intense emotions can narrow attention, disrupt concentration, and reduce problem-solving capacity. For example, a student who becomes overwhelmed by anxiety during assessments may struggle to recall learned concepts, even when they are well prepared. In contrast, emotionally regulated students can acknowledge stress without being dominated by it, allowing them to remain focused and engaged in the task at hand.

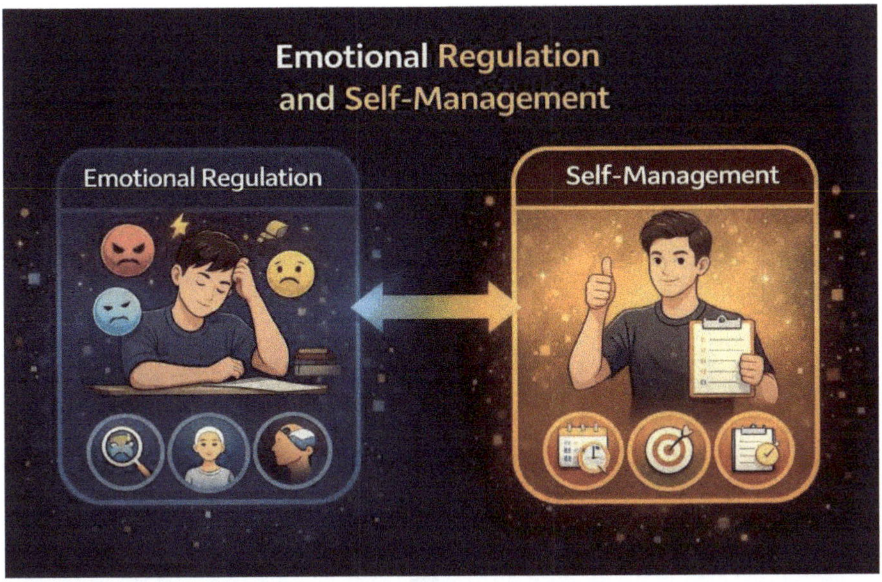

From a psychological perspective, emotional regulation supports cognitive flexibility, resilience, and adaptability. When students learn to pause, reflect, and reframe emotional experiences, they develop greater perseverance and confidence. These abilities are particularly important in skill-based learning environments that require practice, feedback, and gradual improvement. Counselling interventions play a vital role by helping students recognize emotional triggers, challenge unhelpful thought patterns, and adopt healthier coping strategies. Through guided reflection and supportive dialogue, counselling empowers learners to manage emotions effectively, thereby enhancing academic performance, personal growth, and long-term self-development.

5.2 Empathy and Social Awareness

Empathy involves understanding others' emotions, perspectives, and needs. In collaborative learning and workplace environments, empathy enhances communication, teamwork, and leadership. Skill development is increasingly social in nature, requiring cooperation and adaptability.

Empathy and social awareness are vital competencies that enable individuals to understand, relate to, and interact effectively with others. Empathy involves the ability to recognize and appreciate the emotions, perspectives, and experiences of people around us. Social awareness builds on empathy by helping individuals interpret social cues, respect differences, and respond appropriately within group settings. Together, these skills form the foundation for meaningful interpersonal relationships and effective collaboration.

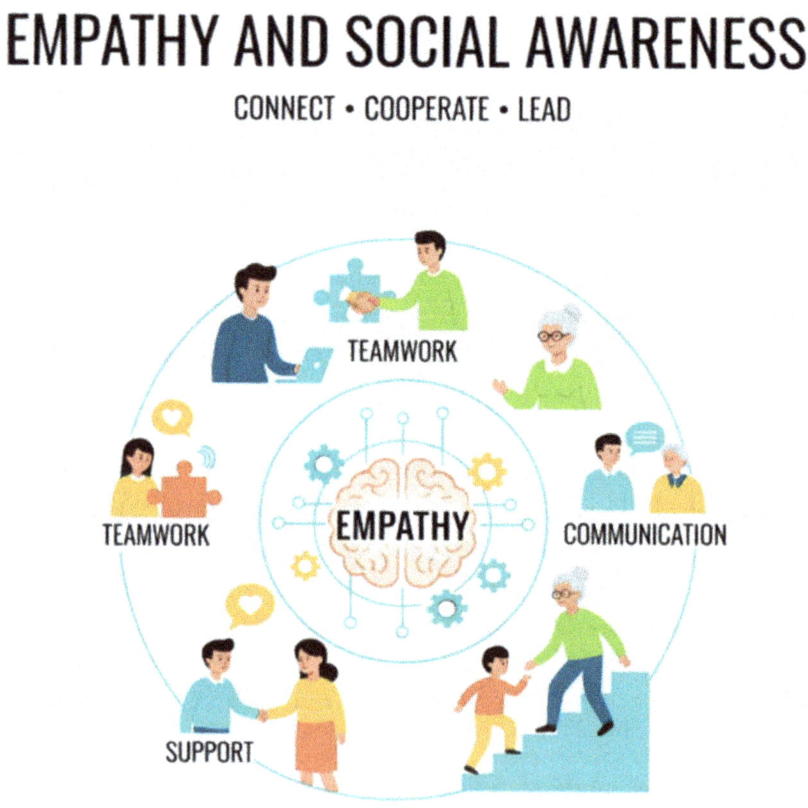

In educational settings, learning is increasingly collaborative, requiring students to work in teams, participate in discussions, and engage in shared problem-solving. Empathetic students are better equipped to listen actively, value diverse viewpoints, and contribute constructively to group tasks. In workplace environments, empathy enhances communication, trust, and leadership by allowing individuals to anticipate others' needs and respond with sensitivity. Leaders who demonstrate empathy foster inclusive cultures where cooperation and mutual respect thrive.

Skill development today extends beyond individual performance to collective success. Projects often demand coordination, adaptability, and conflict management. Students who lack social awareness may struggle with misunderstandings, interpersonal tension, or ineffective teamwork. Counselling plays a crucial role in nurturing empathy and social awareness by helping students reflect on their interactions, recognize emotional signals in others, and develop respectful communication strategies. Through counselling support, learners gain the confidence to navigate group dynamics, resolve conflicts peacefully, and function effectively in diverse academic and professional environments, preparing them for socially complex real-world situations.

5.3 Emotional Intelligence as an Employability Skill

Employers increasingly value emotional intelligence alongside technical competence. Skills such as emotional control, interpersonal sensitivity, and ethical judgment influence professional success. Psychology recognizes emotional intelligence as a predictor of job performance, leadership potential, and career sustainability.

Emotional intelligence has emerged as a critical employability skill in modern professional environments, complementing technical knowledge and domain-specific expertise. Emotional intelligence refers to the ability to understand one's own emotions, manage them effectively, recognize emotions in others, and respond with empathy and sound judgment. As workplaces become more collaborative, diverse, and fast-paced, these emotional capabilities significantly influence how individuals perform, adapt, and grow in their careers.

Employers increasingly seek professionals who can remain composed under pressure, communicate clearly, and work harmoniously with colleagues from varied backgrounds. Skills such as emotional self-control, interpersonal sensitivity, ethical awareness, and constructive conflict management directly affect productivity and workplace relationships. An employee who can regulate stress, accept feedback positively, and respond thoughtfully to challenges is more likely to sustain performance and earn trust within teams. Psychological research consistently identifies emotional intelligence as a strong indicator of job effectiveness, leadership potential, and long-term career stability.

Beyond technical proficiency, emotional intelligence supports decision-making, problem-solving, and ethical conduct in complex situations. Counselling-centric education plays a pivotal role in nurturing these competencies by embedding emotional awareness, reflection, and interpersonal skill development into learning processes. Through guided counselling, students learn to recognize emotional patterns, improve communication, and develop resilience. This integrated approach prepares learners to handle real-world professional challenges with confidence and maturity, ensuring they are not only academically capable but also emotionally equipped for sustainable employability.

5.4 Counselling Strategies to Build Emotional Intelligence

Counselling strategies such as emotional labelling, reflective dialogue, role-playing, and feedback interpretation help students strengthen emotional intelligence. These approaches encourage emotional literacy and resilience.

Counselling plays a crucial role in strengthening emotional intelligence by equipping students with practical strategies to understand and manage emotions effectively. Emotional intelligence is not an innate trait alone; it can be developed through guided reflection, experiential learning, and consistent practice. Counselling-based interventions create a supportive space where students can explore emotional experiences without fear of judgment and gradually build emotional competence.

One effective strategy is **emotional labelling**, which helps students identify and name their emotions accurately. By learning to distinguish between feelings such as stress, frustration, disappointment, or anxiety, students gain clarity over their emotional states and reduce emotional overwhelm. **Reflective dialogue** further deepens this awareness by encouraging students to examine the reasons behind their emotions and evaluate how these feelings influence behaviour and decision-making. This process enhances self-awareness and promotes emotional regulation.

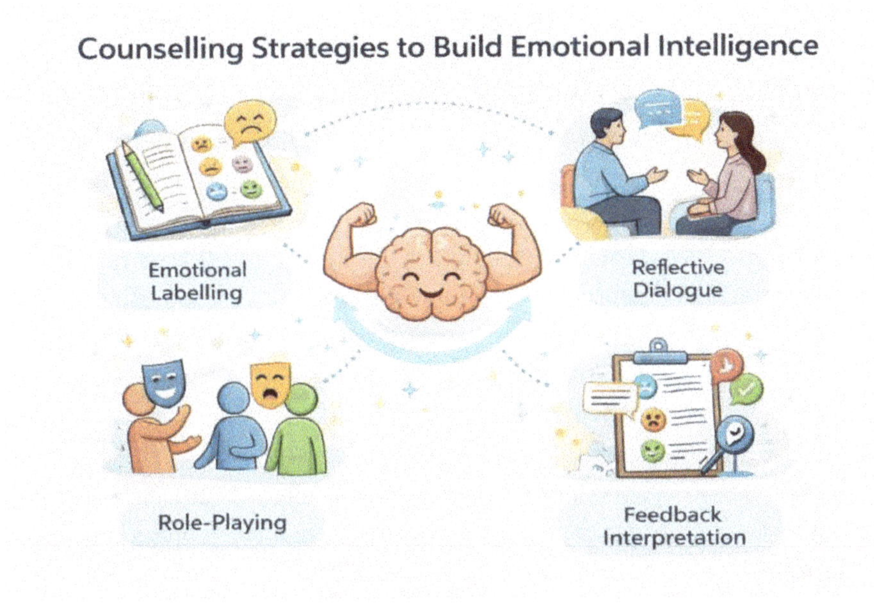

Counselling Strategy	Description	Emotional Intelligence Skills Developed	Practical Outcomes for Students
Emotional Labelling	Guiding students to accurately	Self-awareness,	Reduced emotional

	identify and name their emotions in different situations	emotional clarity	confusion, better emotional control
Reflective Dialogue	Structured conversations that help students reflect on emotional triggers, thoughts, and behaviours	Self-regulation, insight, ethical judgment	Improved decision-making and emotional balance
Role-Playing	Simulated real-life scenarios such as conflict resolution, teamwork, or feedback situations	Empathy, social awareness, adaptability	Enhanced interpersonal skills and confidence
Feedback Interpretation	Teaching students to process criticism constructively rather than defensively	Emotional control, growth mindset	Better response to evaluation and continuous improvement
Stress Response Training	Counselling techniques focused on managing pressure, uncertainty, and performance anxiety	Resilience, emotional stability	Increased coping capacity in academic and professional settings

Role-playing is another valuable counselling tool that allows students to practice responding to real-life situations such as peer conflict, performance pressure, or workplace communication challenges. Through simulated interactions, students develop empathy, adaptability, and appropriate emotional responses. Additionally, **feedback interpretation** helps learners process criticism constructively rather than defensively, fostering growth-oriented thinking. Collectively, these counselling strategies nurture emotional literacy, resilience, and self-control. With guided practice, students learn to respond positively to stress, uncertainty, and evaluation-conditions that are common in both educational settings and professional environments-thereby strengthening emotional intelligence for long-term personal and career development.

Multiple Choice Questions (MCQs)

1. Emotional regulation primarily helps students to:

a) Avoid academic responsibilities
b) Suppress emotions completely
c) Manage emotions to remain focused and adaptive
d) Reduce learning effort

Correct Answer: c) Manage emotions to remain focused and adaptive

2. Which of the following best describes empathy in skill development contexts?

a) Competing aggressively with peers
b) Understanding and responding to others' emotions and perspectives
c) Ignoring group dynamics
d) Focusing only on personal success

Correct Answer: b) Understanding and responding to others' emotions and perspectives

3. Emotional intelligence is increasingly valued by employers because it:

a) Replaces technical skills
b) Eliminates workplace stress
c) Enhances teamwork, leadership, and adaptability
d) Guarantees promotions

Correct Answer: c) Enhances teamwork, leadership, and adaptability

4. Which counselling strategy helps students practice emotional responses in real-life situations?

a) Emotional labelling
b) Role-playing
c) Memorization
d) Passive observation

Correct Answer: b) Role-playing

5. Counselling-centric education contributes to skill development by:

a) Focusing only on academic grades
b) Limiting student interaction
c) Integrating emotional intelligence with learning processes
d) Reducing student autonomy

Correct Answer: c) Integrating emotional intelligence with learning processes

Short Answer Questions

1. What is emotional regulation, and why is it important for skill development?
2. Define empathy and explain its role in collaborative learning environments.
3. How does emotional intelligence contribute to employability?

4. Mention any two counselling strategies used to develop emotional intelligence in students.
5. What is meant by social awareness in the context of emotional intelligence?
6. How does counselling help students manage stress and feedback effectively?

Long Answer Questions

1. Explain the concept of emotional intelligence and discuss its significance in academic and professional skill development.
2. Analyse the role of emotional regulation and self-management in enhancing learning outcomes among students.
3. Discuss empathy and social awareness as essential components of teamwork and leadership in modern workplaces.
4. Examine how counselling-based educational approaches support the development of emotional intelligence.
5. Evaluate the importance of emotional intelligence as an employability skill in today's competitive job market.
6. Describe various counselling strategies used to build emotional intelligence and explain how they prepare students for real-world challenges.

6

Learning Barriers and Psychological Blocks

6.1 Fear of Failure and Performance Anxiety

Fear of failure is one of the most common psychological barriers in skill development. Students may avoid challenges to protect self-esteem, leading to stagnation. Performance anxiety further disrupts concentration and confidence.

Fear of failure is a powerful psychological barrier that often prevents students from reaching their full potential. When learners associate mistakes with personal inadequacy, they tend to avoid difficult tasks, new skills, or competitive situations. This avoidance creates a cycle in which limited effort leads to limited growth, reinforcing the belief that one is incapable. Over time, such patterns can result in academic stagnation and reduced motivation.

Performance anxiety further intensifies this challenge. Under pressure-such as examinations, presentations, or public evaluations-students may experience racing thoughts, physical tension, and difficulty concentrating. Even well-prepared individuals can underperform when anxiety overwhelms their cognitive resources. From a psychological perspective, this anxiety is frequently rooted in unrealistic standards, fear of judgment, and deeply held negative self-beliefs formed through past experiences or social comparisons.

Counselling and psychological support play a crucial role in addressing these issues. Through guided reflection and cognitive restructuring, students learn to view mistakes as natural and necessary steps in the learning process rather than as indicators of failure. Supportive interventions also help learners set realistic goals, develop self-compassion, and build confidence through gradual exposure to challenges. When fear is reframed as feedback rather than failure, students become more resilient, willing to take risks, and capable of sustained personal and academic growth.

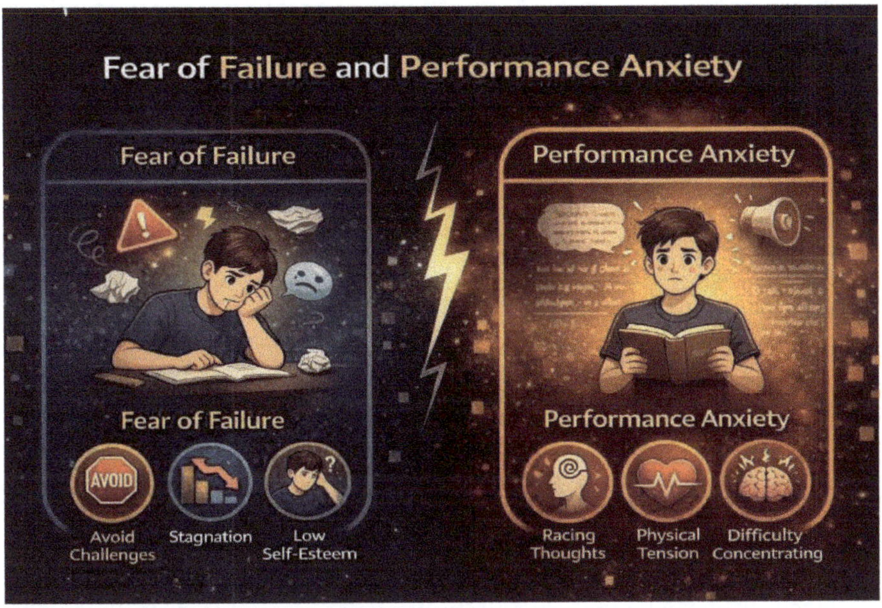

6.2 Procrastination and Avoidance Behaviour

Procrastination is rarely a time-management issue; it is often rooted in emotional discomfort, perfectionism, or fear of evaluation. Avoidance temporarily reduces anxiety but ultimately undermines skill growth.

Procrastination is commonly misunderstood as a simple lack of discipline or poor time management. In reality, it is often driven by deeper psychological factors such as emotional discomfort, fear of failure, perfectionism, or anxiety about being evaluated. When a task feels overwhelming or threatens self-worth, students may delay starting it as a way to escape uncomfortable emotions. This avoidance provides short-term relief but strengthens long-term stress and self-doubt.

Avoidance behaviour gradually interferes with skill development. Each postponed task reduces opportunities for practice, feedback, and improvement, leading to rushed performance or incomplete learning. Over time, this pattern reinforces negative beliefs such as "I work best under pressure" or "I'm not capable," even though the real issue lies in emotional resistance rather than ability.

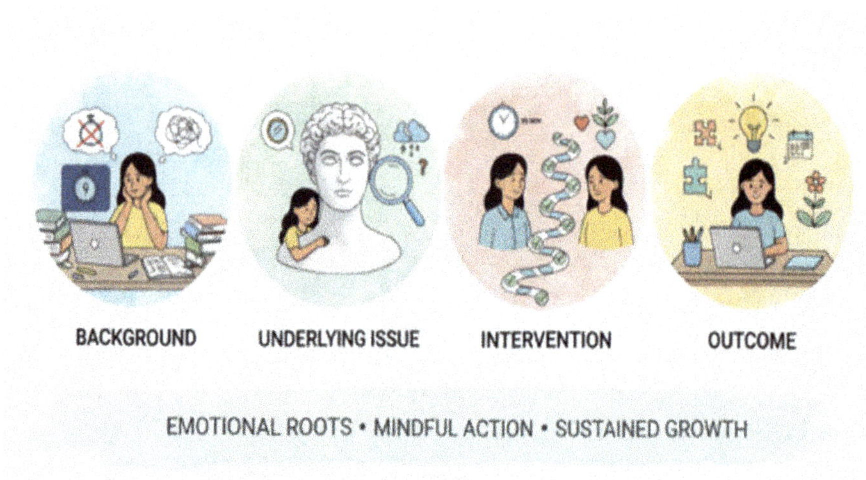

Counsellors play a key role in helping students break this cycle. By guiding learners to identify the emotional triggers behind procrastination, counselling makes the behaviour more understandable and manageable. Students are supported in developing structured, realistic routines that emphasize progress over perfection. Techniques such as task breakdown, time-blocking, and self-reward systems reduce emotional overwhelm and build consistency. When students learn to engage with tasks despite discomfort, procrastination decreases and confidence in their skills steadily improves.

Case Study: Overcoming Procrastination and Avoidance Behaviour

Background

Riya, a 19-year-old undergraduate student, consistently postponed assignments and exam preparation despite being academically capable. She often waited until the last moment to begin tasks, resulting in stress, poor sleep, and performance below her potential. Faculty feedback described her work as "rushed but insightful," which further frustrated her.

Underlying Issue

During counselling sessions, it became clear that Riya's procrastination was not due to poor time management. She struggled with perfectionism and a strong fear of negative evaluation. She believed that if her work was not perfect, it would reflect poorly on her intelligence. To avoid this discomfort, she delayed starting tasks, temporarily reducing anxiety.

Intervention

The counsellor helped Riya identify the emotional triggers behind her avoidance. Together, they reframed tasks as learning opportunities rather than judgments of worth. A structured routine was introduced, breaking assignments into small, low-pressure steps with realistic deadlines. She was encouraged to begin work for just 20 minutes daily, regardless of outcome, and to practice self-compassion instead of self-criticism.

Outcome

Within two months, Riya showed consistent engagement with her coursework. Her anxiety reduced significantly, and she began submitting assignments on time. More importantly, she reported increased confidence and a healthier relationship with effort and failure. The case illustrates how addressing emotional roots-rather than focusing only on time management-can effectively reduce procrastination and support sustained skill development.

6.3 Low Self-Esteem and Learned Helplessness

Low self-esteem weakens motivation and persistence, while learned helplessness leads students to believe that effort will not change outcomes.

Low self-esteem and learned helplessness are deeply interconnected psychological barriers that significantly hinder skill development. Students with low self-esteem often underestimate their abilities, doubt their worth, and interpret setbacks as proof of personal inadequacy. As a result, they may avoid challenges, give up quickly, or rely excessively on external validation, which weakens motivation and persistence over time.

Learned helplessness develops when individuals repeatedly experience failure or perceive a lack of control over outcomes. After multiple negative experiences, students may begin to believe that effort is meaningless, assuming that no matter how hard they try, results will remain unchanged. This belief leads to passivity, reduced initiative, and emotional withdrawal from learning tasks. Even when opportunities for success are present, such students may not attempt them, reinforcing a cycle of inaction and low confidence.

Counselling interventions are essential in breaking this cycle. Counsellors help students recognize and challenge negative self-perceptions while guiding them toward achievable, short-term goals that create experiences of success. Positive reinforcement strengthens confidence, while gradual exposure to manageable challenges rebuilds resilience. Over time, these strategies restore a sense of agency, enabling students to view effort as impactful and competence as developable. As self-belief improves, students become more engaged, motivated, and capable of sustained skill growth.

6.4 Therapeutic and Counselling Interventions

Counselling provides targeted interventions such as cognitive restructuring, confidence-building exercises, stress-management techniques, and supportive goal planning. These methods address emotional and cognitive barriers directly rather than forcing skill practice prematurely.

Intervention Type	Focus Area	Psychological Barrier Addressed	Impact on Skill Development
Cognitive Restructuring	Identifying and modifying negative thought patterns	Fear of failure, self-doubt, irrational beliefs	Improves confidence, enhances persistence, supports positive learning attitudes
Confidence-Building Exercises	Strength recognition and self-efficacy development	Low self-esteem, self-criticism	Encourages risk-taking, increases motivation, strengthens belief in ability
Stress-Management Techniques	Emotional regulation and relaxation strategies	Performance anxiety, chronic stress	Improves concentration, reduces mental overload, supports sustained effort
Supportive Goal Planning	Structured, achievable goal setting	Overwhelm, avoidance, lack of direction	Promotes consistency, builds momentum, enables gradual skill mastery
Emotional Awareness Training	Understanding emotional triggers and responses	Procrastination, avoidance behaviour	Enhances self-regulation, improves task engagement

Gradual Exposure to Challenges	Controlled exposure to difficulty	Learned helplessness, fear-based avoidance	Restores sense of agency, builds resilience and competence

Therapeutic and counselling interventions play a crucial role in supporting students who struggle with emotional and cognitive barriers to learning. Rather than focusing immediately on performance or skill practice, counselling addresses the internal challenges that interfere with engagement, motivation, and confidence. This approach recognizes that unresolved psychological stress can undermine even the most structured academic efforts.

One key method used in counselling is **cognitive restructuring**, which helps students identify and challenge unhelpful thought patterns such as self-doubt, fear of failure, or catastrophizing outcomes. By replacing negative beliefs with balanced and realistic perspectives, students gain greater emotional stability and clarity. **Confidence-building exercises**, including strengths recognition and success reflection, further reinforce positive self-perception and self-efficacy.

Counselling also incorporates **stress-management techniques** such as relaxation strategies, mindfulness, and emotional regulation skills to help students cope with academic pressure. In addition, **supportive goal planning** enables learners to set achievable, step-by-step objectives aligned with their emotional readiness and capacity. These goals emphasize progress over perfection, reducing overwhelm and resistance.

By resolving internal psychological blocks first, counselling creates a safe and supportive foundation for learning. Students become more open to challenges, more resilient in the face of setbacks, and better equipped for sustained skill acquisition and academic growth. **Multiple Choice Questions (MCQs)**

1. Fear of failure primarily affects learning by:

A. Increasing competition among students
B. Encouraging risk-taking behaviour
C. Leading students to avoid challenging tasks
D. Improving concentration under pressure

Answer: C

2. Procrastination is best understood as:

A. Poor time management alone
B. Lack of intelligence
C. A response to emotional discomfort and fear of evaluation
D. Laziness and lack of motivation

Answer: C

3. Learned helplessness develops when students:

A. Set extremely high academic goals
B. Repeatedly experience success
C. Believe effort does not influence outcomes
D. Receive excessive academic support

Answer: C

4. Performance anxiety most directly interferes with:

A. Long-term memory formation
B. Physical health only
C. Concentration and confidence during evaluation
D. Social interaction outside academics

Answer: C

5. Counselling interventions support skill development mainly by:

A. Forcing repeated practice regardless of emotions
B. Ignoring emotional factors and focusing on discipline
C. Addressing psychological barriers before skill practice
D. Replacing academic instruction with therapy

Answer: C

Short Answer Questions

1. What is meant by fear of failure in the context of student learning?
2. Explain how performance anxiety affects academic performance.
3. Why is procrastination considered an emotional issue rather than a time-management problem?
4. Define learned helplessness and its impact on student motivation.

5. How does low self-esteem influence skill development?
6. Mention any two counselling strategies used to overcome psychological learning barriers.

Long Answer Questions

1. Discuss fear of failure and performance anxiety as psychological barriers to skill development.
2. Examine the emotional and cognitive causes of procrastination and avoidance behaviour among students.
3. Explain the concept of learned helplessness and describe how it restricts academic growth.
4. Analyse the relationship between low self-esteem and motivation in the learning process.
5. Describe the role of counselling interventions in addressing psychological blocks to learning.
6. Using suitable examples, explain how counselling can help students regain confidence and agency in academic settings.

7

Cognitive Skills and Critical Thinking

7.1 Problem-Solving and Decision-Making Skills

Problem-solving involves identifying issues, evaluating options, and selecting appropriate solutions, while decision-making focuses on choosing among alternatives under uncertainty. These cognitive skills are essential for academic success and workplace performance.

Problem-solving and decision-making are core cognitive skills that shape how individuals respond to academic challenges and real-world situations. Problem-solving refers to the ability to recognize a challenge, understand its nature, and systematically work toward a solution. Decision-making, on the other hand, involves selecting the most suitable option from several alternatives, often in situations where information is incomplete or outcomes are uncertain. Together, these skills enable individuals to move from confusion to clarity and from indecision to purposeful action.

From a psychological perspective, effective problem-solving relies on logical reasoning, mental flexibility, and emotional regulation. Logical reasoning allows individuals to analyse facts, recognize patterns, and apply prior knowledge to new situations. Flexibility of thought helps in exploring multiple approaches rather than rigidly adhering to a single method. Emotional regulation plays an equally important role, as anxiety, frustration, or fear of failure can block clear thinking and lead to impulsive or avoidance-based decisions.

In educational contexts, students who develop strong problem-solving skills are better equipped to handle complex tasks that require analysis rather than rote memorization. For example, a student facing difficulty with a challenging assignment may learn to divide the problem into smaller, manageable parts, examine each component carefully, and test different solution strategies. This approach not only improves academic performance but also builds confidence and independence in learning.

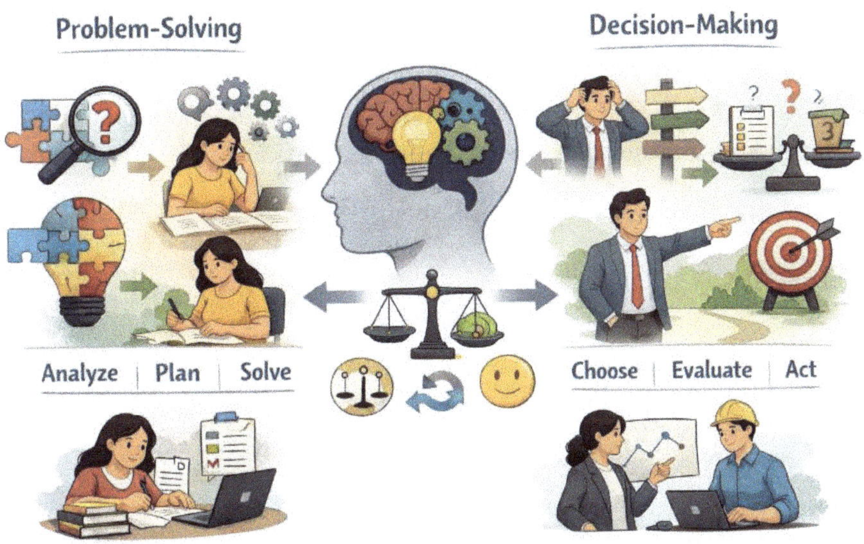

In the workplace, decision-making skills are crucial for managing responsibilities, prioritizing tasks, and responding to unexpected situations. Individuals who can weigh pros and cons, anticipate consequences, and remain calm under pressure are more likely to make balanced and effective choices. Over time, consistent practice of problem-solving and decision-making enhances critical thinking, adaptability, and resilience, making these skills essential for personal growth, professional success, and responsible participation in society.

7.2 Metacognition and Reflective Learning

Metacognition refers to "thinking about one's own thinking." It allows students to monitor their understanding, recognize errors, and adjust learning strategies. Reflective learners actively evaluate what worked and what did not.

Metacognition refers to an individual's awareness and understanding of their own thinking and learning processes. It involves the ability to plan how to approach a task, monitor comprehension while learning, and evaluate the effectiveness of strategies after completing an activity. Rather than focusing only on *what* is learned, metacognition emphasizes *how* learning takes place. This self-awareness enables learners to become more intentional, independent, and effective in their academic efforts.

LEARN FROM EXPERIENCE •
GROWTH MINDSET

Reflective learning is closely linked to metacognition. Reflective learners regularly pause to examine their experiences, asking questions such as what strategies worked well, where difficulties arose, and why certain approaches were successful or unsuccessful. This reflection transforms mistakes into learning opportunities instead of sources of discouragement. By analysing their own thought processes, students develop the capacity to adapt their methods rather than repeating ineffective habits.

From a psychological and counselling perspective, metacognitive awareness is actively nurtured through guided reflection. Counselling shifts the learner's attention away from grades or outcomes alone and toward understanding patterns of thinking, emotional responses, and study behaviours. When students reflect with support, they begin to see learning as a process that can be refined, not a fixed ability they either possess or lack.

For example, a student who performs poorly in an examination may initially attribute failure to lack of intelligence or bad luck. Through reflective discussion with a counsellor, the student reviews specific errors, identifies gaps in understanding, and recognizes unproductive study techniques. By adjusting strategies-such as adopting active recall, better time management, or concept mapping-the student experiences gradual improvement. This process not only enhances academic performance but also builds confidence, self-efficacy, and a growth-oriented mindset that supports lifelong learning.

7.3 Development of Critical Thinking Abilities

Critical thinking involves analysis, evaluation, and logical judgment rather than passive acceptance of information. Students trained in critical thinking question assumptions, identify biases, and draw reasoned conclusions.

Critical thinking refers to the ability to actively analyse information, evaluate evidence, and make reasoned judgments rather than accepting ideas at face value. It moves learners beyond memorization toward deeper understanding, enabling them to question assumptions, recognize underlying patterns, and assess the validity of arguments. In an academic setting, critical thinking empowers students to engage with knowledge thoughtfully instead of passively reproducing information from textbooks or lectures.

From a psychological standpoint, critical thinking develops through deliberate cognitive engagement. Skills such as comparison, inference, evaluation, and logical reasoning are strengthened when learners are encouraged to ask “why” and “how,” not just “what.” Exposure to multiple viewpoints plays a crucial role, as it challenges existing beliefs and reduces cognitive rigidity. When students encounter perspectives different from their own, they learn to examine biases-both in sources of information and in their own thinking.

Guided questioning is a key method for nurturing critical thinking. Teachers and facilitators who pose open-ended, reflective questions prompt students to justify their opinions, examine evidence, and consider alternative explanations. This process helps learners move from surface-level understanding to analytical depth. Over time, students begin to internalize this questioning approach and apply it independently across subjects and real-life situations.

For example, in a classroom discussion structured around reflective questioning, students may be asked to evaluate the strengths and weaknesses of an argument rather than summarize it. Instead of repeating textbook content, they analyse claims, identify assumptions, and support conclusions with logical reasoning. Such practices enhance intellectual independence, improve problem-solving capacity, and prepare students to navigate complex academic, social, and professional challenges with clarity and discernment.

7.4 Role of Counsellors in Cognitive Skill Training

Counsellors support cognitive skill development by teaching reflective techniques, goal-based thinking, and error analysis. They help students

understand how emotions influence reasoning and decision-making. Through counselling sessions, learners develop structured thinking habits that enhance academic learning and workplace adaptability.

Counsellors play a vital role in strengthening students' cognitive skills by guiding them toward more structured, aware, and adaptive thinking patterns. Rather than focusing only on emotional support, counselling actively contributes to the development of reflective thinking, problem-solving abilities, and effective decision-making. Through systematic guidance, counsellors help learners understand how they think, learn, and respond to challenges.

Counsellor Intervention Area	Description	Cognitive Skills Developed	Impact on Learners
Reflective Techniques	Counsellors guide students to review learning	Self-awareness, metacognition,	Improved understanding of learning

	experiences, identify strengths, and recognize mistakes constructively	analytical thinking	processes and reduced fear of failure
Goal-Based Thinking	Students are trained to set realistic goals, break tasks into steps, and track progress	Planning, organization, strategic thinking	Enhanced focus, motivation, and task completion
Error Analysis	Counsellors help learners analyse errors without self-blame and identify causes	Logical reasoning, evaluation, adaptability	Better learning from mistakes and continuous improvement
Emotional Regulation Support	Counsellors address anxiety, stress, and emotional barriers affecting cognition	Emotional control, judgment, decision-making	Clearer thinking and improved performance under pressure
Decision-Making Guidance	Learners are supported in weighing options and anticipating consequences	Reasoned judgment, responsibility	Balanced and informed decision-making in academics and life

One key contribution of counsellors is teaching reflective techniques. These include reviewing past experiences, identifying successful strategies, and recognizing patterns of error or avoidance. By encouraging students to reflect on *how* they approached a task rather than only *what* result they achieved, counsellors promote deeper learning and continuous improvement. Goal-based thinking is another important area, where students are helped to set realistic objectives, break them into achievable steps, and monitor progress over time.

Counsellors also assist students in understanding the connection between emotions and cognition. Anxiety, stress, fear of failure, or low self-esteem can significantly affect reasoning, concentration, and judgment. Through counselling, learners become aware of these emotional influences and learn strategies to regulate them, such as reframing negative thoughts or adopting calm, logical responses under pressure. This emotional awareness supports clearer thinking and more balanced decision-making.

Over repeated counselling sessions, students gradually develop disciplined thinking habits. They learn to analyse mistakes without self-blame, adapt strategies when outcomes are unsatisfactory, and approach new challenges with confidence and flexibility. These cognitive skills not only enhance academic performance but also prepare learners for workplace environments that demand adaptability, critical reasoning, and thoughtful decision-making. In this way, counsellors contribute meaningfully to both educational success and long-term personal and professional development.

Multiple Choice Questions (MCQs)

1. Which of the following best defines problem-solving skills?

   a) Memorizing information for examinations
   b) Identifying problems and applying suitable strategies to resolve them
   c) Following instructions without questioning
   d) Repeating learned solutions without analysis

Correct Answer: b) Identifying problems and applying suitable strategies to resolve them

2. Metacognition is most accurately described as:

a) Learning through repetition
b) Thinking about one's own thinking and learning processes
c) Emotional intelligence alone
d) Passive observation of information

Correct Answer: b) Thinking about one's own thinking and learning processes

3. Which practice best promotes critical thinking in students?

a) Rote memorization of textbook content
b) Teacher-centred lectures only
c) Guided questioning and discussion of multiple perspectives
d) Frequent testing without feedback

Correct Answer: c) Guided questioning and discussion of multiple perspectives

4. How do counsellors contribute to cognitive skill development?

a) By focusing only on academic grades
b) By discouraging reflection on mistakes
c) By teaching reflective techniques and emotional regulation
d) By replacing classroom teaching

Correct Answer: c) By teaching reflective techniques and emotional regulation

5. Emotional regulation is important for decision-making because it:

a) Eliminates the need for logical reasoning
b) Encourages impulsive choices
c) Helps manage stress that can impair judgment
d) Prevents learning from mistakes

Correct Answer: c) Helps manage stress that can impair judgment

Short Answer Questions

1. Define problem-solving skills and explain their importance in academic learning.
2. What is metacognition? State any two benefits of metacognitive awareness for students.
3. How does reflective learning differ from rote learning?
4. Mention any two characteristics of critical thinking.
5. How do emotions influence decision-making according to psychology?
6. State the role of counsellors in improving students' cognitive skills.

Long Answer Questions

1. Explain the concept of problem-solving and decision-making skills. Discuss their relevance in both academic and workplace contexts.
2. Describe metacognition and reflective learning. How do these processes help students improve their learning strategies and confidence?
3. Critically examine the development of critical thinking abilities in students. What teaching methods support this development?
4. Discuss the psychological factors involved in effective decision-making. How can emotional regulation enhance reasoning abilities?
5. Explain the role of counselling in cognitive skill training. Highlight how counsellors help learners develop structured thinking habits.
6. Evaluate the importance of cognitive skills and critical thinking for lifelong learning and adaptability in a rapidly changing world.

8

Social Skills and Communication Psychology

8.1 Interpersonal Skills and Teamwork

Interpersonal skills include cooperation, listening, negotiation, and conflict management. In collaborative environments, these skills determine how effectively individuals work with others. Psychology emphasizes that social competence is learned through interaction and feedback.

Interpersonal skills are the social and emotional abilities that enable individuals to interact effectively with others. These include cooperation, active listening, empathy, negotiation, adaptability, and conflict management. In any collaborative setting-such as classrooms, workplaces, or community initiatives-these skills play a decisive role in determining how smoothly and productively a group functions. Technical knowledge alone is not sufficient for collective success; the ability to understand others' perspectives, express ideas clearly, and manage differences constructively is equally essential.

From a psychological standpoint, interpersonal competence is not innate but developed over time through social interaction, observation, and continuous feedback. Individuals learn how to interpret social cues, regulate emotions, and respond appropriately by engaging with peers in diverse situations. Constructive feedback helps people recognize the impact of their behaviour on others, refine communication styles, and develop mutual respect. This learning process strengthens self-awareness and emotional intelligence, which are critical for teamwork.

In educational and professional environments, structured group activities provide a practical context for nurturing these skills. When group projects are supported by reflective feedback-such as peer reviews or guided discussions-participants become more conscious of their communication patterns and collaborative roles. For example, students working in teams learn to distribute responsibilities fairly, listen to differing viewpoints, and resolve disagreements without hostility. Over time, such experiences foster a culture of trust and shared accountability, preparing individuals to work effectively in diverse, team-oriented environments.

8.2 Communication Psychology and Expression

Effective communication involves clarity, emotional awareness, and adaptability to context. Psychological factors such as confidence, fear of judgment, and cultural background influence communication styles. Communication psychology examines how thoughts, emotions, and social contexts shape the way individuals express themselves and interpret others. Effective communication is not limited to speaking fluently; it involves clarity of ideas, emotional awareness, and the ability to adapt messages according to audience, situation, and purpose. Psychological readiness plays a crucial role-individuals must feel emotionally secure and cognitively organized to communicate with confidence and authenticity.

Several psychological factors influence communication styles. Confidence affects voice modulation, eye contact, and message coherence, while fear of judgment can lead to hesitation, avoidance, or excessive self-monitoring. Cultural background further shapes communication by influencing norms related to assertiveness, politeness, silence, and non-verbal expression. As a result, two individuals with similar knowledge may communicate very differently based on their psychological conditioning and social experiences.

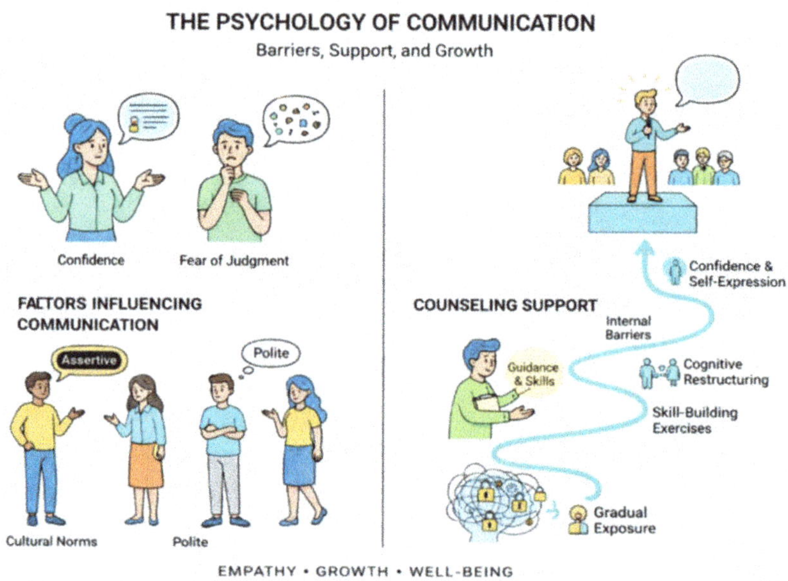

Counselling plays a supportive role in strengthening communication by addressing internal barriers such as anxiety, low self-esteem, or negative self-beliefs. Through guided reflection and skill-building exercises, students learn to recognize irrational fears, regulate emotional responses, and practice assertive expression. Techniques such as role-playing, cognitive restructuring, and gradual exposure help individuals gain confidence in safe, structured settings.

For instance, a student experiencing stage fear may initially struggle with public speaking due to anticipatory anxiety and fear of embarrassment. With counselling-supported practice-starting with small group discussions and gradually progressing to larger audiences-the student builds confidence incrementally. Over time, repeated exposure combined with positive reinforcement transforms anxiety into self-assurance, leading to improved presentation skills and more effective self-expression.

8.3 Assertiveness and Confidence Building

Assertiveness enables individuals to express opinions and needs respectfully without aggression or withdrawal. Many students struggle to balance confidence with politeness. Psychology explains assertiveness as a learned behaviour shaped by self-belief and emotional control. Assertiveness is the ability to express one's thoughts, feelings, and needs clearly and respectfully while acknowledging the rights and perspectives of others. It lies between two ineffective extremes-aggression, which disregards others, and passivity, which suppresses one's own voice. For students, developing assertiveness is essential for academic participation, healthy relationships, and future professional interactions.

Many learners struggle to maintain this balance between confidence and politeness. Cultural expectations, fear of rejection, low self-esteem, or past negative experiences often lead students to avoid speaking up or, conversely, to communicate in a defensive manner. Psychology views assertiveness as a learned behaviour rather than an inherent trait. It is shaped by self-belief, emotional regulation, and an individual's perception of personal worth. When students believe their opinions have value and can manage anxiety or frustration, assertive communication becomes more natural.

Confidence building is closely linked to assertiveness. As individuals gain confidence, they are more likely to express themselves without excessive fear or self-doubt. Psychological approaches focus on increasing self-awareness, challenging negative self-talk, and strengthening emotional control. This enables students to respond thoughtfully rather than react impulsively in challenging situations.

Practical strategies such as role-play exercises are highly effective in developing assertiveness. By simulating academic discussions, group negotiations, or professional interactions, students can practice expressing disagreement, making requests, or setting boundaries in a supportive environment. Feedback during these exercises helps refine tone, body language, and word choice. Over time, repeated practice reinforces confidence and equips students with the skills to communicate assertively and respectfully across diverse contexts.

8.4 Counselling Students for Social Adaptability

Counsellors guide students in understanding social cues, managing conflicts, and adapting to diverse environments. Through reflective discussion and behavioural rehearsal, counselling enhances social intelligence. This adaptability is critical for employability, leadership, and professional growth.

Social adaptability refers to an individual's capacity to adjust behaviour, communication, and emotional responses according to different social situations and interpersonal dynamics. In rapidly changing academic, professional, and multicultural environments, this ability has become essential. Counselling plays a significant role in developing social adaptability by helping students understand social cues, interpret others' emotions, and respond appropriately in varied contexts.

Counsellors work with students to increase social awareness and emotional insight through reflective discussion. By exploring real-life interactions, students learn to recognize non-verbal signals such as tone, facial expressions, and body language, which are often as important as spoken words. Counselling also addresses challenges like misunderstanding, social anxiety, and interpersonal conflict by helping individuals identify triggers and evaluate alternative responses. This reflective process strengthens self-regulation and empathy, two core components of social intelligence.

Behavioural rehearsal is another key counselling technique used to enhance adaptability. Through guided practice, students rehearse responses to common social and professional scenarios such as teamwork disagreements, interviews, leadership roles, or cross-cultural interactions. Repeated practice in a safe, non-judgmental environment allows students to experiment with different behaviours, build confidence, and internalize adaptive strategies.

Social adaptability developed through counselling has long-term benefits beyond academic life. It directly contributes to employability by improving collaboration, communication, and conflict-resolution skills valued by employers. Furthermore, adaptable individuals are better equipped for leadership and professional growth, as they can navigate diverse teams, manage change effectively, and build positive relationships across organizational and cultural boundaries.

Multiple Choice Questions (MCQs)

1. Which of the following best describes interpersonal skills in a collaborative environment?

A. Technical expertise required for task completion
B. Ability to dominate group discussions
C. Skills related to cooperation, listening, and conflict management
D. Individual performance without group interaction

Correct Answer: C

2. According to communication psychology, which factor most strongly influences an individual's communication style?

A. Academic qualification
B. Psychological factors such as confidence and fear of judgment
C. Physical appearance
D. Speed of speech alone

Correct Answer: B

3. Assertiveness is best defined as the ability to:

A. Avoid expressing opinions to maintain harmony
B. Express opinions aggressively to prove authority
C. Express thoughts and needs respectfully without aggression or withdrawal
D. Always agree with others in group situations

Correct Answer: C

4. How does counselling support the development of social adaptability?

A. By enforcing strict behavioural rules
B. By focusing only on academic performance
C. By guiding reflection, understanding social cues, and practicing

adaptive behaviours
D. By reducing social interactions

Correct Answer: C

5. Why is social adaptability considered critical for employability and leadership?

A. It replaces technical skills entirely
B. It helps individuals avoid teamwork
C. It enables effective collaboration, conflict resolution, and adjustment to diverse environments
D. It limits interaction to familiar social groups

Correct Answer: C

Short Answer Questions

1. What are interpersonal skills, and why are they important in teamwork?
2. How do psychological factors influence communication styles?
3. Define assertiveness and explain how it differs from aggression.
4. What role does counselling play in reducing communication anxiety?
5. Explain the concept of social adaptability in simple terms.
6. Why is reflective feedback important in developing social skills?

Long Answer Questions

1. Discuss the role of interpersonal skills in effective collaboration within academic and professional environments.
2. Explain communication psychology and analyse how emotions, confidence, and cultural background affect self-expression.

3. Describe assertiveness as a learned behaviour and examine its relationship with confidence building among students.

4. Evaluate the role of counselling in enhancing social adaptability and social intelligence.

5. Analyse how role-play and behavioural rehearsal contribute to the development of communication and assertiveness skills.

6. Examine the importance of social skills and communication psychology for employability, leadership, and long-term professional growth.

9

Resilience, Stress Management, and Adaptability

9.1 Stress Psychology and Coping Mechanisms

Stress is a natural psychological response to perceived challenges or demands. While moderate stress can enhance performance, excessive stress impairs learning and health. Psychology identifies coping mechanisms such as problem-focused and emotion-focused strategies.

Stress is a common psychological experience that arises when individuals perceive a situation as demanding or overwhelming. It is not always harmful. In moderate amounts, stress can motivate learners, sharpen focus, and improve performance by encouraging effort and alertness. However, when stress becomes intense or prolonged, it negatively affects concentration, memory, emotional balance, and physical health, thereby hindering effective learning and overall well-being.

Psychology explains stress through the interaction between external pressures (such as examinations, deadlines, or expectations) and an individual's ability to cope with them. When demands exceed perceived coping capacity, stress levels increase. To manage this, individuals rely on coping mechanisms-conscious strategies used to handle stressful situations.

Coping mechanisms are broadly classified into **problem-focused coping** and **emotion-focused coping**. Problem-focused strategies aim to address the source of stress directly. These include time management, goal setting, seeking academic help, and planning tasks systematically. Emotion-focused strategies, on the other hand, help regulate emotional responses to stress. Techniques such as deep breathing, mindfulness, relaxation exercises, positive self-talk, and social support fall under this category.

In educational settings, teaching students effective coping skills is essential. For example, guiding students to create structured study plans reduces uncertainty and workload pressure, while relaxation and breathing exercises help manage exam anxiety. By developing healthy coping mechanisms, learners become more resilient, emotionally balanced, and better equipped to handle academic and life challenges.

9.2 Building Resilience in Students

Resilience refers to the ability to recover from setbacks and persist despite difficulties. It develops through supportive environments, self-belief, and adaptive coping strategies. Counselling helps students view challenges as growth opportunities rather than personal failures. Psychological resilience refers to an individual's capacity to adapt, recover, and continue functioning positively despite experiencing stress, failure, or adversity. Rather than avoiding difficulties, resilient individuals learn to face challenges with flexibility and determination. In educational contexts, resilience plays a crucial role in helping students manage academic pressure, setbacks, and uncertainty without losing motivation or self-confidence.

Resilience is not an inborn trait; it develops gradually through life experiences and supportive environments. Key contributors include encouragement from teachers and family, a sense of belonging, realistic goal-setting, and the development of self-belief. When students feel supported and valued, they are more likely to view obstacles as temporary and manageable rather than overwhelming. Adaptive coping strategies-such as problem-solving, emotional regulation, and seeking guidance-further strengthen resilience by enabling students to respond constructively to stress.

Counselling plays a significant role in building psychological resilience. Through reflective dialogue and guided support, counselling helps students reframe challenges as learning experiences rather than personal shortcomings. It encourages self-awareness, emotional balance, and the ability to learn from failure. Students gradually shift from self-blame to self-growth, fostering a healthier academic mindset.

Case Illustration: A student experiencing repeated academic setbacks may begin to doubt their abilities. With counselling support, the student is guided to reassess goals, identify strengths, and adopt realistic strategies for improvement. Over time, confidence is rebuilt, persistence increases, and setbacks are viewed as stepping stones toward personal and academic growth.

9.3 Adaptability in Changing Environments

Adaptability involves adjusting behaviour and mindset in response to new demands. In rapidly changing academic and professional contexts, adaptability is a critical survival skill. Psychology highlights cognitive flexibility and emotional openness as key components.

Adaptability refers to the ability to adjust one's thinking, behaviour, and emotional responses when faced with new conditions, challenges, or expectations. In today's rapidly evolving academic and professional environments, adaptability has become an essential life skill. Continuous technological change, shifting career paths, and interdisciplinary knowledge demands require individuals to move beyond rigid habits and embrace flexibility in learning and problem-solving.

From a psychological perspective, adaptability is closely linked to **cognitive flexibility** and **emotional openness**. Cognitive flexibility allows individuals to shift perspectives, modify strategies, and consider alternative solutions when familiar approaches no longer work. Emotional openness enables individuals to tolerate uncertainty, manage discomfort, and remain receptive to new experiences rather than resisting change. Together, these qualities support effective adjustment in unfamiliar or demanding situations.

In educational settings, adaptable students are better equipped to handle curriculum changes, diverse learning formats, and evolving assessment methods. They are more willing to learn new skills, integrate knowledge across disciplines, and respond constructively to feedback. Adaptability also reduces anxiety, as students who expect change are less threatened by it and more confident in their ability to cope.

Example: Students engaged in multidisciplinary learning-such as combining science, technology, arts, and social sciences-develop broader thinking patterns and transferable skills. This exposure helps them adapt more easily to new academic expectations and emerging professional roles, preparing them for lifelong learning in dynamic environments.

9.4 Counselling Models for Emotional Strength

Counselling models emphasize emotional awareness, cognitive reframing, and stress regulation. These approaches strengthen emotional endurance and decision-making under pressure. Counselling ensures that students develop resilience not through avoidance but through healthy engagement with challenges.

Counselling Model / Approach	Core Focus	Key Techniques Used	Emotional Strength Outcomes
Emotional Awareness–Based Counselling	Understanding and identifying emotions	Self-reflection, emotional labelling, guided discussions	Improved self-awareness, emotional clarity, reduced suppression
Cognitive Reframing Approach	Changing negative thought patterns	Challenging irrational beliefs, positive reinterpretation	Better decision-making, reduced anxiety, realistic thinking

Stress Regulation Counselling	Managing emotional pressure effectively	Relaxation techniques, mindfulness, breathing exercises	Emotional stability, calmness under pressure
Problem-Solving Counselling	Active engagement with challenges	Goal setting, structured planning, solution mapping	Confidence, persistence, constructive coping
Resilience-Oriented Counselling	Growth through adversity	Reflective dialogue, strengths identification	Emotional endurance, adaptability, self-belief

Counselling models play a vital role in strengthening emotional health by helping individuals understand, manage, and respond constructively to their emotions. Emotional strength does not imply the absence of stress or difficulty; rather, it reflects the capacity to remain balanced, thoughtful, and resilient when facing pressure. In educational contexts, counselling supports students in developing this strength by fostering self-awareness and healthy emotional regulation.

Most counselling approaches emphasize **emotional awareness**, which enables students to recognize and name their feelings instead of suppressing or ignoring them. By understanding emotional triggers and responses, students gain greater control over their reactions. **Cognitive reframing** is another key element, helping individuals challenge negative or distorted thought patterns and replace them with more realistic and constructive perspectives. This shift improves decision-making and reduces emotional overwhelm during challenging situations.

Stress regulation techniques form a core component of counselling models. Practices such as guided reflection, relaxation exercises, mindfulness, and structured problem-solving help students maintain emotional stability under academic and social pressure. Rather than encouraging avoidance, counselling promotes healthy engagement with challenges, teaching students to face difficulties with confidence and clarity.

Through consistent counselling support, students learn that resilience is built through experience, reflection, and adaptation. They develop emotional endurance, improved judgment, and the ability to respond calmly to setbacks, preparing them to navigate both academic demands and future life challenges with strength and self-assurance.

Multiple Choice Questions (MCQs)

1. Which of the following best defines psychological resilience?

a) Avoiding stressful situations completely
b) Suppressing emotional responses to challenges
c) Recovering from setbacks and continuing to function effectively
d) Ignoring failures and focusing only on success

Correct Answer: c) Recovering from setbacks and continuing to function effectively

2. Moderate levels of stress are considered beneficial because they:

a) Eliminate emotional responses
b) Reduce the need for preparation
c) Enhance motivation and focus
d) Prevent academic challenges

Correct Answer: c) Enhance motivation and focus

3. Problem-focused coping strategies primarily aim to:

a) Regulate emotional reactions
b) Avoid stressful situations

c) Address the source of stress directly
d) Increase emotional dependence

Correct Answer: c) Address the source of stress directly

4. Cognitive flexibility, a key component of adaptability, refers to the ability to:

a) Maintain rigid thinking patterns
b) Shift perspectives and adjust strategies
c) Eliminate emotional responses
d) Rely only on past experiences

Correct Answer: b) Shift perspectives and adjust strategies

5. Counselling contributes to emotional strength mainly by:

a) Encouraging avoidance of challenges
b) Promoting emotional suppression
c) Supporting healthy engagement and cognitive reframing
d) Reducing academic responsibilities

Correct Answer: c) Supporting healthy engagement and cognitive reframing

Short Answer Questions

1. Define psychological resilience.
2. What is stress, and how can moderate stress be beneficial?
3. Mention any two coping mechanisms used to manage stress.
4. What is meant by adaptability in changing environments?
5. Explain cognitive flexibility in brief.
6. State the role of counselling in managing academic stress.

Long Answer Questions

1. Discuss the concept of stress and explain different coping mechanisms used to manage it.
2. Explain the importance of psychological resilience in students' academic and personal lives.
3. Analyse how adaptability helps individuals succeed in rapidly changing educational and professional environments.
4. Describe the role of counselling models in developing emotional strength and resilience among students.
5. Examine the relationship between stress management, emotional regulation, and effective decision-making.
6. Illustrate with suitable examples how counselling helps students transform academic setbacks into growth opportunities.

References

Chapter 1: Introduction to Skill Development Psychology

- Anderson, J. R. (1982). Acquisition of cognitive skill. *Psychological Review*, 89(4), 369–406.
- Fitts, P. M., & Posner, M. I. (1967). *Human Performance*. Belmont, CA: Brooks/Cole.
- Ericsson, K. A., Krampe, R. T., & Tesch-Römer, C. (1993). The role of deliberate practice in the acquisition of expert performance. *Psychological Review*, 100(3), 363–406.
- National Education Policy (NEP). (2020). *Ministry of Education, Government of India.*

Chapter 2: Understanding the Student Mind

- Piaget, J. (1972). *The Psychology of the Child*. New York: Basic Books.
- Vygotsky, L. S. (1978). *Mind in Society: The Development of Higher Psychological Processes*. Harvard University Press.
- Steinberg, L. (2014). *Age of Opportunity: Lessons from the New Science of Adolescence*. Houghton Mifflin Harcourt.
- Bruner, J. S. (1996). *The Culture of Education*. Harvard University Press.

Chapter 3: Motivation and Skill Acquisition

- Deci, E. L., & Ryan, R. M. (2000). Intrinsic and extrinsic motivations: Classic definitions and new directions. *Contemporary Educational Psychology*, 25(1), 54–67.
- Locke, E. A., & Latham, G. P. (2002). Building a practically useful theory of goal setting and task motivation. *American Psychologist*, 57(9), 705–717.

- Bandura, A. (1997). *Self-Efficacy: The Exercise of Control*. New York: Freeman.
- Schunk, D. H., Meece, J. L., & Pint rich, P. R. (2014). *Motivation in Education: Theory, Research, and Applications*. Pearson.

Chapter 4: Self-Awareness and Skill Identity

- Rogers, C. R. (1961). *On Becoming a Person*. Boston: Houghton Mifflin.
- Super, D. E. (1990). A life-span, life-space approach to career development. *Journal of Vocational Behaviour*, 16(3), 282–298.
- Holland, J. L. (1997). *Making Vocational Choices: A Theory of Vocational Personalities and Work Environments*. Psychological Assessment Resources.

Chapter 5: Emotional Intelligence and Skill Development

- Goleman, D. (1995). *Emotional Intelligence*. New York: Bantam Books.
- Mayer, J. D., Salovey, P., & Caruso, D. R. (2004). Emotional intelligence: Theory, findings, and implications. *Psychological Inquiry*, 15(3), 197–215.
- Bar-On, R. (2006). The Bar-On model of emotional-social intelligence. *Psicothema*, 18, 13–25.
- OECD. (2015). *Skills for Social Progress: The Power of Social and Emotional Skills*.

Chapter 6: Learning Barriers and Psychological Blocks

- Seligman, M. E. P. (1975). *Helplessness: On Depression, Development, and Death*. Freeman.
- Beck, A. T. (1976). *Cognitive Therapy and the Emotional Disorders*. International Universities Press.

- Steel, P. (2007). The nature of procrastination. *Psychological Bulletin*, 133(1), 65–94.
- Zeidner, M. (1998). *Test Anxiety: The State of the Art*. Springer.

Chapter 7: Cognitive Skills and Critical Thinking

- Halpern, D. F. (2014). *Thought and Knowledge: An Introduction to Critical Thinking*. Psychology Press.
- Flavell, J. H. (1979). Metacognition and cognitive monitoring. *American Psychologist*, 34(10), 906–911.
- Facione, P. A. (2011). *Critical Thinking: What It Is and Why It Counts*. Insight Assessment.

Chapter 8: Social Skills and Communication Psychology

- Argyle, M. (1991). *Cooperation: The Basis of Sociability*. Routledge.
- Bandura, A. (1986). *Social Foundations of Thought and Action*. Prentice-Hall.
- McCroskey, J. C. (1984). The communication apprehension perspective. *Journal of Communication*, 34(3), 78–96.
- Spitzberg, B. H., & Cupach, W. R. (2011). *Interpersonal Skills*. Sage Publications.

Chapter 9: Resilience, Stress Management, and Adaptability

- Lazarus, R. S., & Folkman, S. (1984). *Stress, Appraisal, and Coping*. Springer.
- Masten, A. S. (2001). Ordinary magic: Resilience processes in development. *American Psychologist*, 56(3), 227–238.
- Bonanno, G. A. (2004). Loss, trauma, and human resilience. *American Psychologist*, 59(1), 20–28.

APPENDIX

1. Glossary of Key Terms

- Skill Development: The structured process through which individuals acquire, refine, and apply cognitive, emotional, social, and technical abilities.
- Skill Acquisition Theory: A psychological framework explaining how learners progress from novice to expert through practice and cognitive adaptation.
- Counselling-Centric Education: An educational approach that integrates psychological guidance with academic and skill training.
- Emotional Intelligence (EI): The ability to recognize, regulate, and utilize emotions effectively in oneself and others.
- Metacognition: Awareness and regulation of one's own thinking and learning processes.
- Intrinsic Motivation: Engagement in learning driven by internal interest or satisfaction.
- Extrinsic Motivation: Engagement influenced by external rewards or pressures.
- Resilience: The capacity to recover from setbacks and adapt to challenges.
- Neuroplasticity: The brain's ability to reorganize neural pathways in response to learning and experience.
- Employability Skills: Transferable psychological and social skills that enhance job readiness and workplace success.
- Bloom's Taxonomy: A hierarchical framework describing levels of learning from basic recall to creative synthesis.

- Psychological Readiness: Emotional, cognitive, and motivational preparedness for academic or professional transitions.

2. Data Sources and Datasets

The conceptual and applied foundations of this book draw upon validated and widely used academic and institutional data sources, including:

- National education policy documents and curriculum frameworks
- Longitudinal studies on skill development, learning behaviour, and employability
- Student assessment data from higher education and vocational training contexts
- Psychological scales measuring motivation, emotional intelligence, resilience, and self-efficacy
- Global workforce and future skills report from international organizations
- Peer-reviewed datasets in cognitive psychology, neuroscience, and educational psychology

These sources support evidence-based counselling interventions and learner-centric skill models discussed throughout the book.

3. Tools and Frameworks

The book integrates established psychological, counselling, and educational frameworks, including:

- Fitts and Posner's Three-Stage Model of Skill Learning
- Self-Determination Theory (Motivation)
- Social Cognitive Theory
- Career Development and Life-Span Models

- Emotional Intelligence Models
- Cognitive Behavioural Counselling Techniques
- Stress and Coping Frameworks
- Neuroplasticity-Based Learning Models
- Bloom's Taxonomy (Cognitive, Affective, Psychomotor Domains)
- Employability and Career Readiness Frameworks

These tools are used to bridge theory with practical counselling and skill development strategies.

4. References for Further Reading

Readers seeking deeper exploration may consult the following authoritative works:

- *Skill Acquisition and Expertise Development* in cognitive psychology
- *Educational Psychology and Student Development*
- *Counselling Psychology in Educational Settings*
- *Emotional Intelligence and Workplace Success*
- *Neuroscience of Learning and Memory*
- *Career Development and Employability Studies*
- *Bloom's Taxonomy and Learning Assessment*

These readings complement the theoretical and applied perspectives presented in this book.

5. Future Directions in Psychology of Skill Development

The future of skill development psychology will be shaped by several emerging trends:

- Integration of counselling with AI-assisted learning platforms
- Personalized skill pathways based on psychological profiling
- Expansion of emotional and social skills as core employability indicators
- Increased focus on lifelong learning and career transitions
- Neuroscience-informed education and training methods
- Greater recognition of mental well-being as a prerequisite for skill mastery
- Alignment of educational systems with rapidly evolving workforce demands

Future research and practice will increasingly position counsellors as central facilitators of sustainable human development.

6. Summary of Key Points

- Skill development is a psychological, biological, and social process- not merely technical training.
- Counselling plays a critical role in addressing motivation, emotional regulation, and self-belief.
- Students differ psychologically; inclusive approaches enhance learning outcomes.
- Emotional intelligence, resilience, and adaptability are essential employability skills.
- Biological mechanisms such as neuroplasticity explain how skills are physically formed.
- Bloom's Taxonomy provides a structured roadmap for progressive skill mastery.

About the Author

Kishore Chandrakant Raipurkar is a retired Professor of Mechanical Engineering with over four decades of distinguished experience in higher and technical education under the Government of Maharashtra. He has

served in multiple academic leadership roles including Head of Department, Training and Placement Officer, Controller of Examinations, and In-Charge Principal at reputed government engineering institutions. Holding postgraduate degrees in Mechanical Engineering and Psychology, he uniquely integrates technical expertise with human development, pedagogy, and mentoring. He has designed university curricula, authored academic books, led national-level training programs, and contributed to industry-academia collaboration initiatives. Currently pursuing a Ph.D. in Psychology, he continues to work as a trainer, counselor, and education consultant, with a strong commitment to student employability and social development.

PUBLISH YOUR BOOK WITH DOI

www.books.wissira.us

Your book now will be listed on one of the world's biggest publishing platforms - WISSIRA Press (books.wissira.us).

Your book will be available worldwide, including:

USA, UK, Germany, Italy, Austria, France, Japan, Sweden

🌏 Asian countries and many more.

It will also be distributed across 20+ major global platforms, including Wissira – United States

1. Amazon – United States
2. Apple Books – United States (Apple Inc.)
3. Barnes & Noble – United States
4. BOL (Bol.com) – Netherlands
5. Booktopia – Australia
6. Book.com – United States
7. BOKUS – Sweden (Bokus.com is Swedish)
8. Casadellibro – Spain
9. CULTURA – France (Cultura is a French books / media retailer)

10. E-LIBRAIRIE – France (French online bookstore)
11. Everand – India (Everand Book Distributor is based in India)
12. EXLIBRIS – Switzerland
13. Fable – United Kingdom (UK/Europe digital subscription book service)
14. Flipkart – India
15. GANDHI.com – Mexico (Librerías Gandhi)
16. Google Book – United States (Google LLC)
17. Google Audio Book – United States (Google LLC)
18. IBS.IT – Italy Wikipedia
19. Indigo – Canada
20. Kobo – Canada Wikipedia
21. Kindle – United States (Amazon product)
22. LAFELTRINELLI – Italy Wikipedia
23. Lehmanns – Germany
24. Lulu – United States
25. MORAWA – Austria
26. Rakuten Japan – Japan (Rakuten)
27. Smashwords – United States

28. Tolino / Thalia – Germany (Tolino is a German-language eBook ecosystem, Thalia DE)
29. Vivlio – France
30. Saxo – Denmark (Saxo.com)
31. YES24 – South Korea and others.

📦 You will receive 20 physical author copies FREE to your Indian address.

⭐ You can also receive 5 book reviews:

* 3 reviews by eminent university professors +* 2 reviews from your own group/colleagues/seniors/teachers

www.books.wissira.us

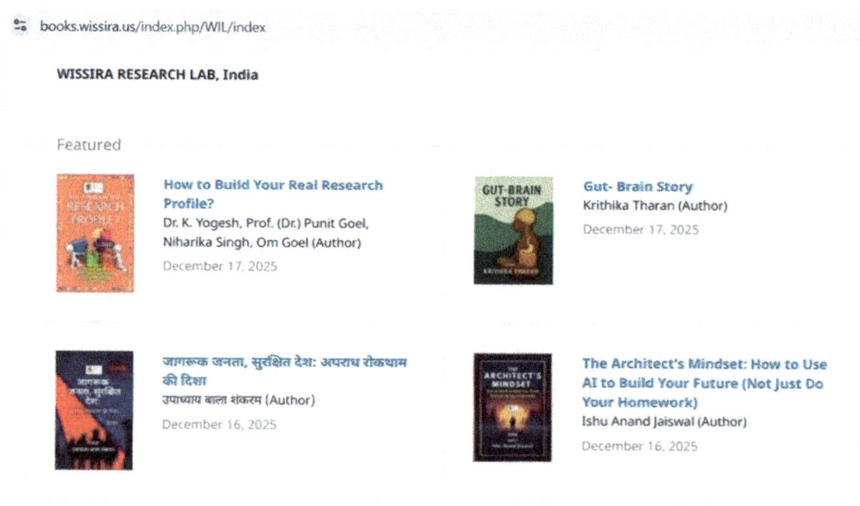

www.books.wissira.us

DOI: https://doi.org/10.63345/book.wrl.2512000324

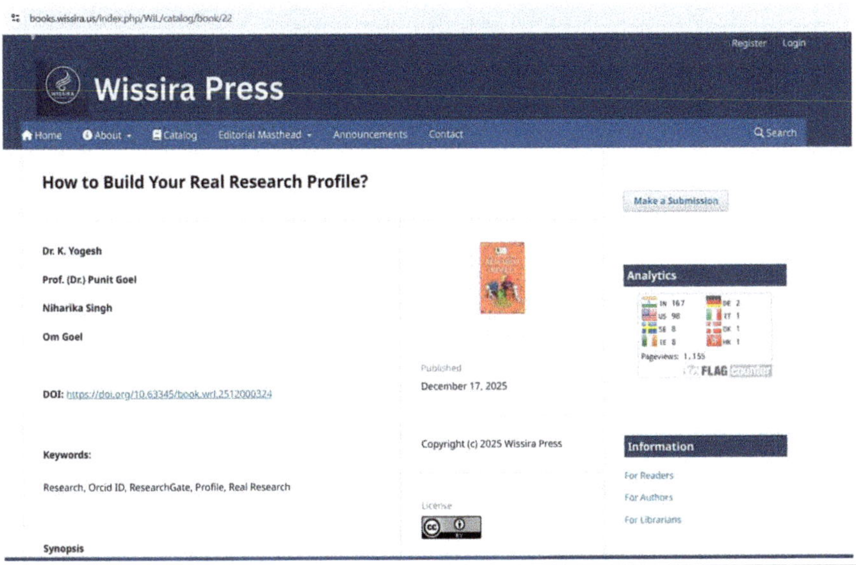

https://books.wissira.us/index.php/WIL/login

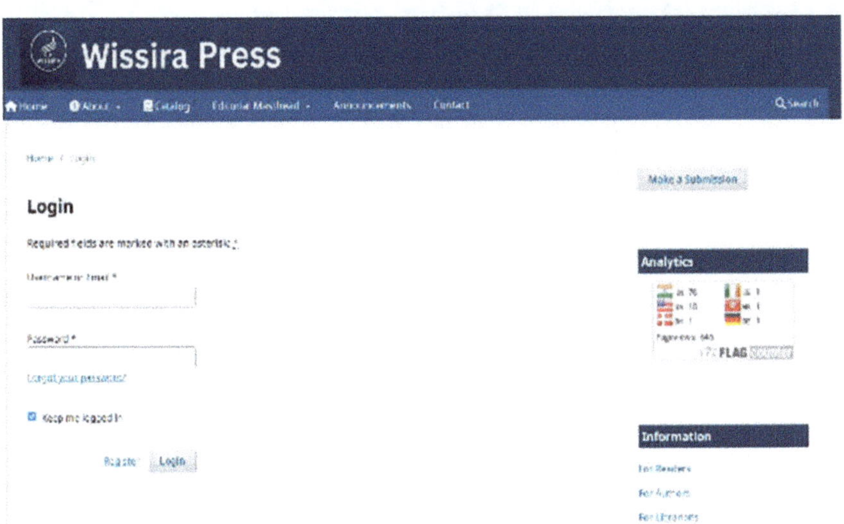

https://books.wissira.us/index.php/WIL/catalog

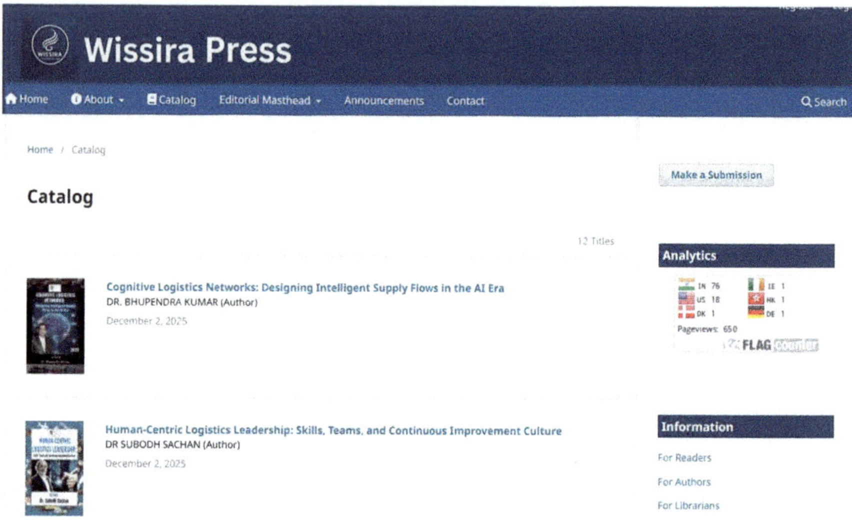

https://books.wissira.us/index.php/WIL/about/contact

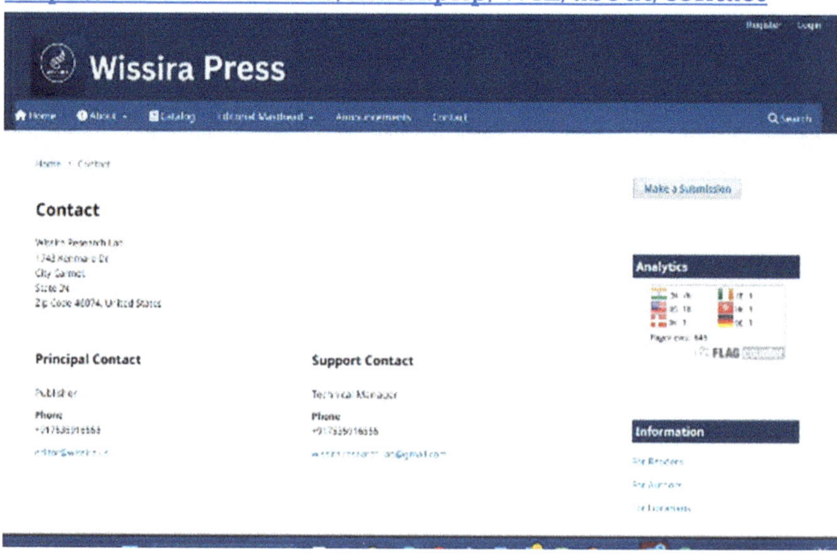

https://www.amazon.in/dp/B0G7MQFD2L

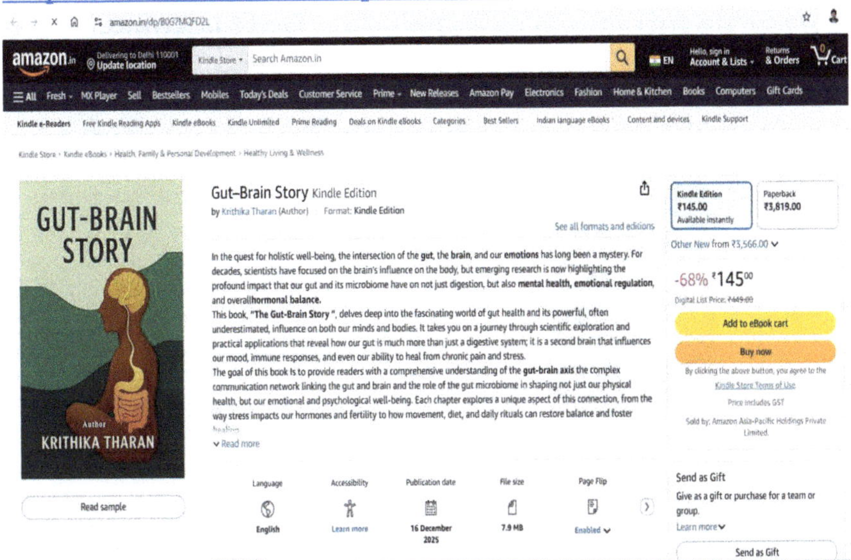

https://books.apple.com/us/book/the-architects-mindset-how-to-use-ai-to-build-your/id6756545876

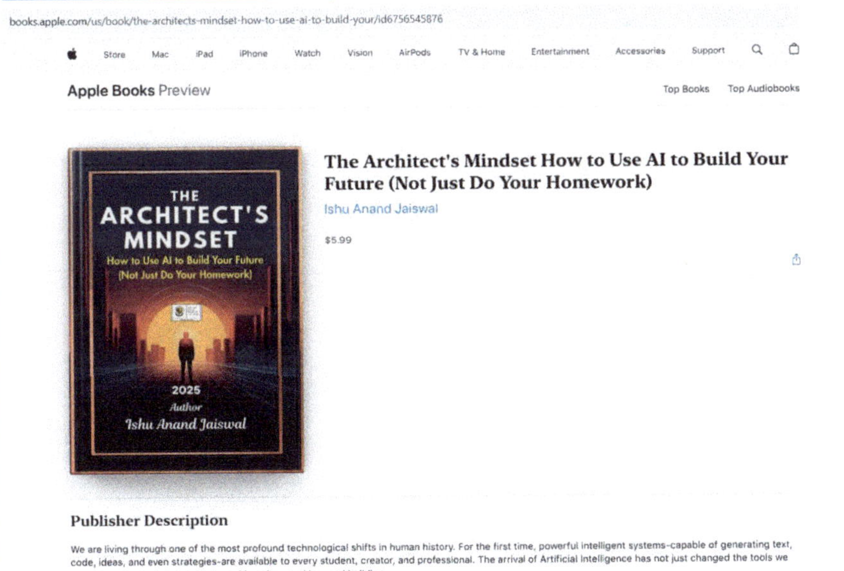

Flipkart:
https://tinyurl.com/WissieaPressBook250306Human

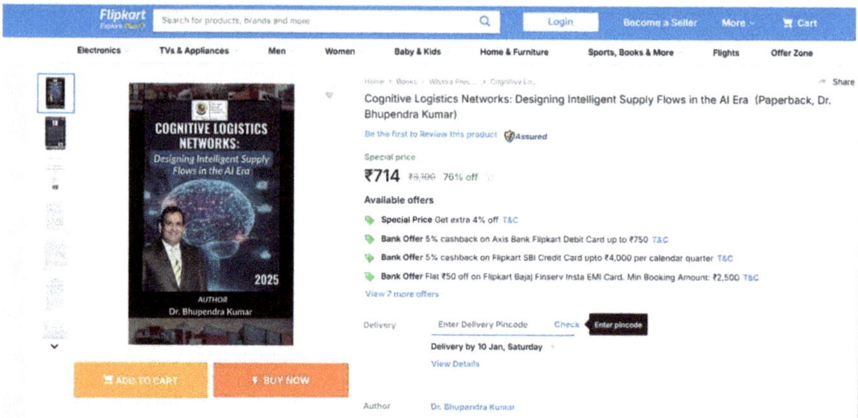

https://shop.vivlio.com/product/9798232547615_9798232547615_10020/human-centric-logistics-leadership-skills-teams-and-continuous-improvement-culture

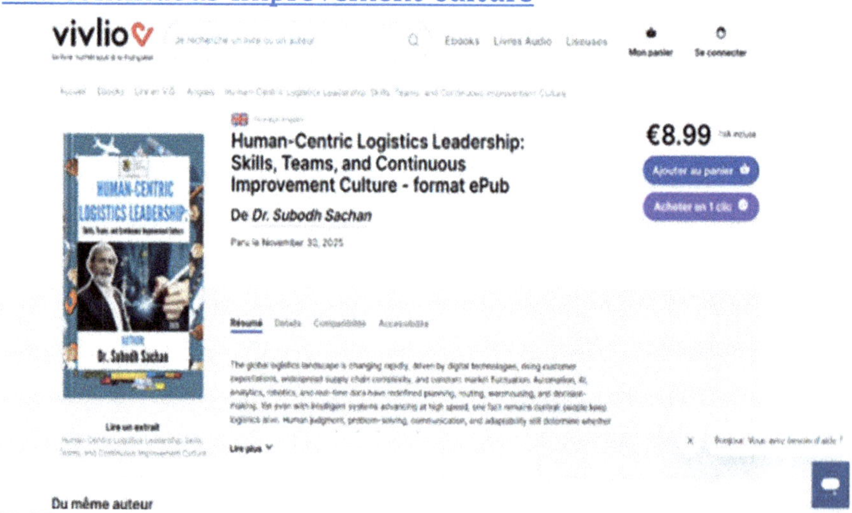

https://fable.co/book/x-9798230804772

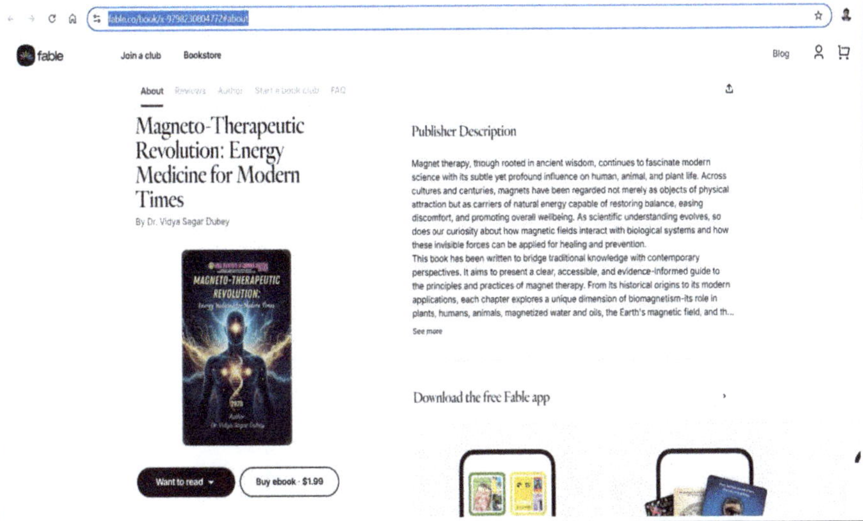

https://www.kobo.com/in/en/ebook/from-shakespeare-to-tagore-reinterpreting-english-literature-through-indian-sensibility?sId=070486d4-8aef-4220-a1d2-26bb2ba8ecb6&ssId=3FJLsnB4eTMdnS31kaTcM

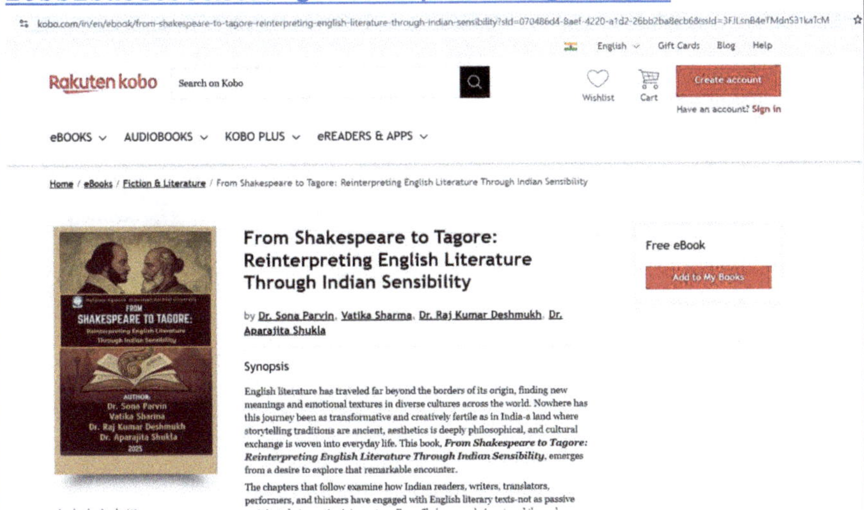

https://www.lulu.com/shop/dr-subodh-sachan/human-centric-logistics-leadership/ebook/product-rmj4erq.html?q=Human-Centric+Logistics+Leadership%3A+Skills%2C+Teams%2C+and+Continuous+Improvement+Culture&page=1&pageSize=

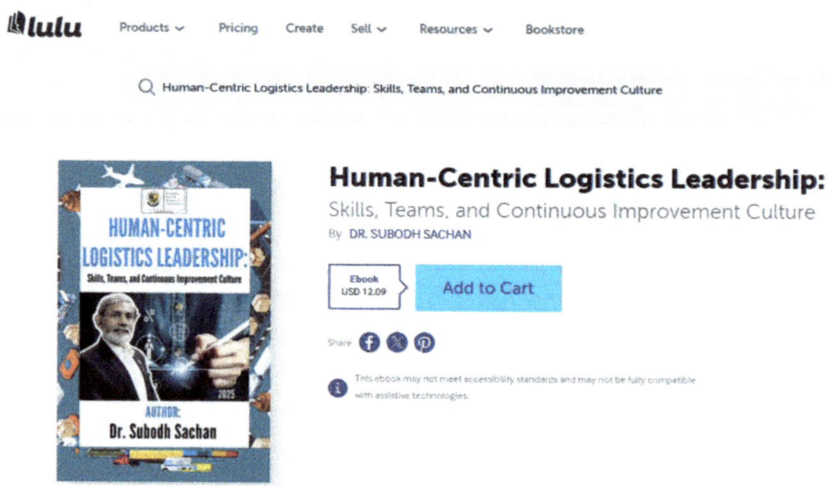

4

https://play.google.com/store/audiobooks/details?id=AQAAAEDqoRHh6M

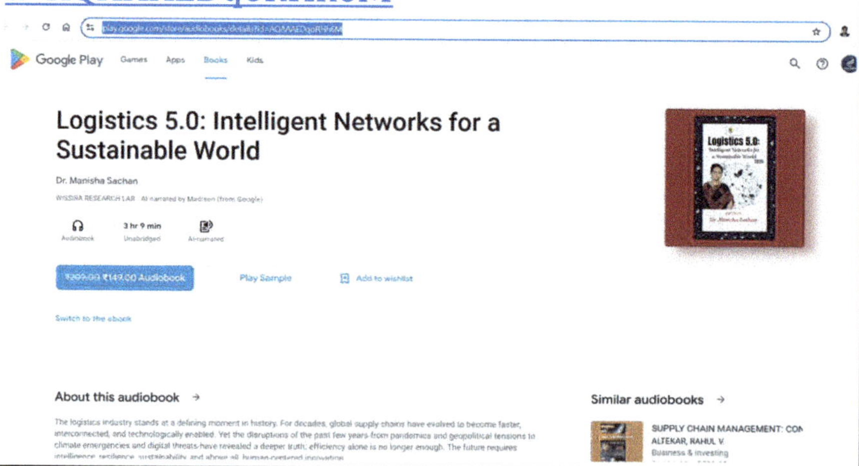

https://play.google.com/store/books/details?id=TbmfEQAAQBAJ

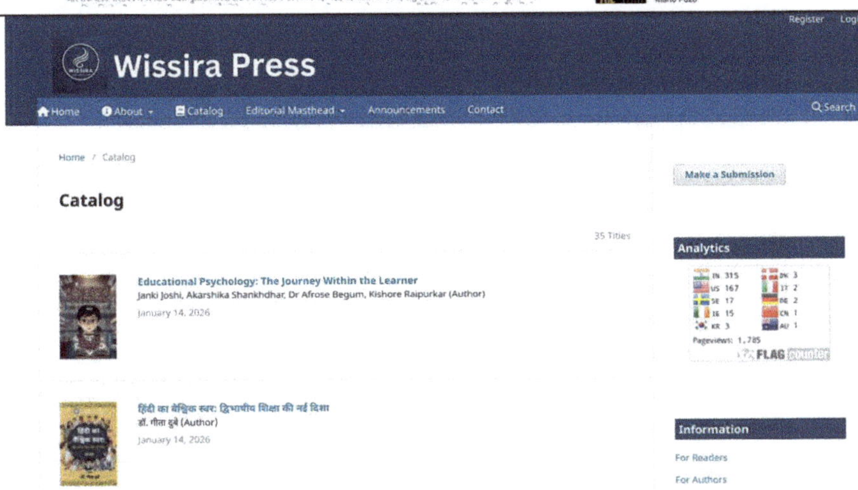

Amazon Kindle

Amazon

Flipkart

LULU

Apple Books

Barnes & Nobles

Everand

Fable

Kobo

Analytics

IN	135	IT	1
US	84	DK	1
SE	8	HK	1
IE	8	DE	1

Pageviews: 1,012

FLAG counter

Information

For Readers

For Authors

For Librarians

Keywords

sustain long-term operational excellence.

Across the nine chapters of this work, readers will find a structured and practical approach to understanding how leadership influences logistics outcomes. Beginning with the foundations of human-centric leadership, the book explores essential competencies such as communication, empathy, decision-making, and ethical responsibility-skills that enable leaders to build credibility and trust in high-pressure environments. It then moves deeper into the dynamics of teamwork, motivation, and empowerment, highlighting how resilient and collaborative teams become the backbone of

Smashwords

Tolino

Vivlio

Google Books

This is a golden opportunity to get global recognition as an author.

You will also enjoy 10–15% lifetime royalty on your book sales.

📨 Expect an official email from editor@wissira.us containing:

* Your Book Publication Certificate

* The ISBN allocation letter from the Government of India

🏆 Your book will also be eligible for nomination for the Best Book Award at the World Book Fair 2027.

👉 Do not miss this opportunity. To publish your book, Connect with us now:

https://wa.me/91753591655

Mob: +911 7535 916 555

---

www.ingramcontent.com/pod-product-compliance
Ingram Content Group UK Ltd.
Pitfield, Milton Keynes, MK11 3LW, UK
UKHW021411190726
13845UKWH00028B/1014

9 789375 592433